Breaking Bad and Cinematic Television

spin offs

A production of the Console-ing Passions book series
Edited by Lynn Spigel

Breaking Bad and Cinematic Television

ANGELO RESTIVO

DUKE UNIVERSITY PRESS *Durham and London* 2019

Printed in the United States of America on acid-free paper ∞
Typeset in Warnock and News Gothic by Tseng Information Systems, Inc.

Library of Congress Cataloging-in-Publication Data
Names: Restivo, Angelo, [date] author.
Title: Breaking bad and cinematic television / Angelo Restivo.
Description: Durham : Duke University Press, 2019. | Series: Spin offs : a production of the Console-ing Passions book series | Includes bibliographical references and index.
Identifiers: LCCN 2018033898 (print)
LCCN 2018043471 (ebook)
ISBN 9781478003441 (ebook)
ISBN 9781478001935 (hardcover : alk. paper)
ISBN 9781478003083 (pbk. : alk. paper)
Subjects: LCSH: Breaking bad (Television program : 2008–2013) | Television series—Social aspects—United States. | Television series—United States—History and criticism. | Popular culture—United States—History—21st century.
Classification: LCC PN1992.77.B74 (ebook) | LCC PN1992.77.B74 R47 2019 (print) | DDC 791.45/72—dc23
LC record available at https://lccn.loc.gov/2018033898

Cover art: *Breaking Bad*, episode 103 (2008).

Duke University Press gratefully acknowledges
the support of Georgia State University's
College of the Arts, School of Film, Media, and
Theatre, and Creative Media Industries Institute,
which provided funds toward the
publication of this book.

Not to mention
that most terrible
drug—ourselves—
which we take
in solitude.

—WALTER BENJAMIN

Contents

note to the reader ix

acknowledgments xi

Introduction 1

1 The Cinematic 25

2 The House 54

3 The Puzzle 81

4 Just Gaming 116

5 Immanence: A Life 137

notes 159

bibliography 171

index 179

Note to the Reader

While this is an academic study, I have tried to write the book in such a way that it will be accessible to the generally educated reader.

The reader need not have had a deep engagement with the series; however, the book presumes a basic familiarity with the characters and larger, overarching story line. Such information is easily available on the web, and I have not prefaced the book with a detailed description of characters or narrative development. Often, I am analyzing single shots or images, or larger recurring stylistic motifs of the series. However, whenever I am describing a scene that seems to require an understanding of the story line leading up to it, I provide the background.

I am hoping that, by the time the book is in print, I will have completed a series of video essays to go along with the argument in chapter 3. Interested readers should go to the Vimeo website and search my name.

Finally: there will be spoilers.

Acknowledgments

If there is anyone without whose encouragement and support this book would not be possible, it is Lynn Spigel. Lynn's work has always been central to the ways I think about cinema, space, and everyday life, and her strong encouragement when I initially spoke to her about this project—many years ago at a Society for Cinema and Media Studies conference, when the project was still only an idea—really helped to get me started in earnest. Since then, she has been a close reader of most of the chapters, and her smart comments have been invaluable.

Much of this book was written under the radar, so to speak, in the sense that I have not been publishing chapters and have presented this material in only a handful of conference talks. Still, many of the ideas in this book developed in conversation with colleagues and friends. In Chicago, once again when this project was in its earliest stages, I remember meeting Lauren Berlant at a café in Hyde Park, and the animated conversation that ensued helped me see that I was onto something. Carl Ulaszek—who in another life was my cinematographer—spent hours with me going over frame grabs from the series as we discussed lighting, camera, and set design. I must also thank Sharon Solwitz and Jeff Sconce.

My friends at *World Picture* always provided a congenial and intellectually challenging venue for thought, and I thank Meghan Sutherland and Brian Price for consistently organizing one of the great "salons" for discussing cutting-edge work in media and theory. And at Rendering (the) Visible, a conference organized by the Moving Image Studies program at Georgia State University (of which I am a part), my thinking benefited from conversations with Amy Villarejo, Amy Herzog, and Eugenie Brinkema. I also thank my friends Kara Keeling and Rich Cante. Finally, Tim Kelley, my friend dating back to our undergraduate years at the University of Chicago, meticulously (and sometimes ruthlessly!) copyedited every single sentence of the manuscript; any stylistic infelicities that remain are entirely my own.

My colleagues in the Moving Image Studies program are a joy to be around, and I must especially thank Alessandra Raengo, Jennifer Barker, and Greg Smith. We are fortunate to have a very smart group of doctoral students, and Justin Horton, John Roberts, Adam Cottrel, Dewey Musante, Jenny Gunn, and Arzu Karaduman kept me on my toes. Graduate research assistants Ella Tucan and Chris Minz provided me with invaluable bibliographic material (and counted beats as well!). Navid Darvishzadeh helped format the index and prepare it for submission. The students in my graduate seminar on *Breaking Bad* shared, each and every week, the results of their own wide-ranging research on the series: thanks to Daren Fowler, Ahmet Yuce, Jason Querry, William Kemp, Michael Bass, Beth Mauldin, and Cameron Hubbard. Finally, special thanks to my grad assistant Reggie Hill, who has been collaborating with me on the video essays that will complement the book.

The color frame grabs would not have been possible without the generous support of Wade Weast, dean of the new College of the Arts; Greg Smith, director of the new School of Film, Media, and Theatre; and David Cheshier, director of the new Creative Media Industries Institute. (The three "new"s in that sentence are evidence there's a lot happening in film and media now at GSU.)

At Duke, I must thank first of all Ken Wissoker for his support. The two outside readers provided me with very smart feedback, and the way the book is contextualized has benefited greatly from their comments. Elizabeth Ault has been an enthusiastic editor: toward the end of the review process, Elizabeth was promoted to full editor, and I was quite honored when she asked whether she could take on this book as one of her first projects in her new position. Finally, Liz Smith copyedited the manuscript with meticulous care; her many suggestions helped streamline the prose, and the book is a better read because of her work.

Much of this book was written in my beloved Chicago, and I must finally thank my friends Cathy Earnest and David Rue for generously opening up to me—sometimes for months at a time!—their beautiful house in Uptown. Cathy and David, together with all the friends who regularly came through for leisurely dinners and wine, are really my second family, and I send them all my love.

Introduction

Considering only its narrative premise, it might seem surprising that the AMC television series *Breaking Bad* (2008–13) became such a strong cultural force that, throughout the mediasphere, we routinely encounter references to the series even today. Ultraviolent and yet suffused with a playful—if dark—humor, the narrative of *Breaking Bad* begins when the mild-mannered and aptly named Walter White, an underpaid yet overqualified high school chemistry teacher in Albuquerque, New Mexico, is suddenly—and ironically, given that he has never smoked—stricken with stage-four lung cancer, with little in the way of financial wherewithal to cover the kind of treatment that his employer-provided health insurance plan would not. After seeing television news footage of a local drug bust, he convinces his brother-in-law, Hank, an agent for the Drug Enforcement Administration (DEA), to let him ride along on the next bust, where he notices one of his ex-students, Jesse Pinkman, escape from the scene. Convinced that he can use his expertise in chemistry to produce a finer-quality meth than anyone on the street has ever seen, Walter blackmails Jesse into partnering with him as he begins a new career as a drug "dealer." This is only the first episode. In the course of the series, we will see the enterprise move from local, artisanal production to a centralized, industrialized production controlled by drug cartels, and finally to the decentralized, just-in-time production characteristic of today's post-Fordist economy. We will see Walter's marriage disintegrate then get reborn as a *mariage de convenance* and business arrangement, only finally to end in utter ruination. We will see Walter and Jesse go through every variation of the father-son relationship, only to have the relationship end with murderous rage and utter contempt. And we will see Walter engage in increasingly brutal acts of violence that slowly detach themselves from the need for self-defense that marks his earliest violent acts.

A dark series indeed. And while the story lines are carefully and cleverly plotted, and no doubt provided much by way of narrative pleasure to the many fans of the series, it was *how* the series presented its story that became the subject of so many critical accolades. In a period that some have characterized as television's third golden age, when innovations in the content and style of dramatic serials were flourishing, *Breaking Bad* seemed to push the expressive possibilities of serial television even farther, by employing expressive devices that were generally considered the province of cinema. This is not to say that cinematic expression was unheard of in television before this point (and I will get to the debates over "cinematic television" in the pages that follow). But *Breaking Bad* was unrelenting in its inventive rethinking of how image and sound might be configured within the televisual system. Indeed, as I will argue, the series seems to be so steeped in the history of cinematic forms that its images often acquire a haunted quality, as if the archive of cinematic expression were hovering in a virtual space just outside every sequence.

This book is an attempt to understand just what this means. And while it might seem that a relentless attention to style over narrative content might lead us to miss the social, cultural, and ultimately political relevance of this series, this study will show that, on the contrary, such an attention to the cinematic (as a concept) can allow us to see how the social and political are treated in the series as purely immanent to our present world. The chapters thus move in ever widening circles: from an examination of how the series presents the domestic spaces and the object world of our contemporary moment, to the ways in which it explores the modes of experience characteristic of neoliberal capitalism, and finally to how a renewed televisual aesthetics can bring us toward a politics of pure immanence. To do this, I bring in ideas from a number of philosophers and theorists, from Walter Benjamin to Gilles Deleuze. I have tried to do so in such a way that the arguments are accessible to nonspecialist readers. And in any case, the moves to theory are always driven by problems presented by the series, in keeping with my fundamental commitment to aesthetics and to immanent critique.

Before the television premiere of the final half season of *Breaking Bad*, the Film Society of Lincoln Center programmed a screening marathon of all the previously aired episodes.[1] For some—especially the proponents of the idea of a second (or a third) golden age of television—this welcoming of a TV series by one of the leading gatekeepers of the world cinematic canon was evidence that a certain kind of television had acquired the cultural prestige heretofore accorded to the cinema. For the purposes of this study, however, this event is better seen as articulating a *problem*: the problem of what a cinematic television might mean. For in the first place, the cultural distinction accorded to the cinema is still only a relatively recent phenomenon, coinciding with the postwar emergence of art cinema, the reorganization of the film canon around the idea of the auteur, and the diffusion of television as a rival to the box office. The cinema's meteoric rise to distinction thus attests to the permeability of judgments of high and low, especially in relation to popular or industrial art. Second, following Lynn Spigel, we can note the ways in which network television even from the beginning aligned itself with modernist values in graphic, industrial, and architectural design. As Spigel's research shows, this led to collaborations between television and the Museum of Modern Art, New York (MoMA), and—perhaps even more telling—the production in the 1950s of a short-lived series called *Point of View*, which attempted to rethink the city films of the 1920s avant-garde cinema for the medium of television.[2] Which is to say that cinematic expression found its way into television early on.

Nonetheless, there is a widely talked-about sense that in the past two decades, some new relationship between cinema and television has been forged, enough to give traction to the phrase "cinematic television." In February 2001, for example, MoMA screened the first two seasons of *The Sopranos*, complemented with a film series curated by *Sopranos* showrunner (and notorious cinephile) David Chase, as if to suggest a new continuity between contemporary television aesthetics and the canon of cinema.[3] Much more recently, in a special feature on the "merging" of film and TV, *Chicago Tribune* television critic Steven Zeitchik suggested that the new blurred boundaries between the media might be better served by "the idea of a more general screen critic."[4] Whether or not one takes *The Sopranos* as paradigmatic, there is nevertheless a wide consensus—among critics and scholars alike—that somewhere around the turn of the century, the nascent forces that had been reshaping the television industry away from the network model finally became visible in the programming.

As early as 2004, in the collection *Television after TV: Essays on a Medium in Transition*, there was a sense among some of the most prominent television scholars that a decisive shift was happening in television. In her introduction to the collection, coeditor Lynn Spigel noted that over the past decade, television had "reinvented itself," and that "in the face of these changes much of the existing literature in television studies now seems as dated as network shows like *Dallas*."[5] Such a reinvention of television involved a conjunction of forces at the levels of industry, economics, technologies, and regulatory regimes, and the now voluminous work (both scholarly and journalistic) on how these factors interacted to produce the kind of television we see today is well beyond the scope of the present study, which will be focused on one aesthetic regime that emerged out of this conjunction. I can, however, sketch out very broadly some of these "conditions of possibility" for a series like *Breaking Bad* (at the risk not only of being reductive but also of stating "what everyone already knows by now"): immersive technologies that allow for greater engagement with the audiovisual sensorium; diversification of viewing practices; new modes of dissemination of product; loosening of restrictions on content; increased economic viability of niche audiences—in short, all those elements that characterize the postnetwork era.[6]

This study will focus on aesthetics: and more specifically, what it means to talk about aesthetics in the context of cinematic television. Aesthetics here is not to be taken as purely formal analysis or as identification of styles or "looks." Rather, it is to be taken in its most far-reaching sense: as the Frankfurt School understood, the formal innovations of the art of an era must be seen as expressive of invisible, macrological shifts in social and economic organization, but also as deeply connected to micrological changes in the experience of everyday life. It is this latter—the imbrication of aesthetic innovation and the lived experience of the everyday—that makes television today an especially fertile ground for aesthetic study. Scholars are beginning to do work in this area—for example, in the section on comedy in the collection *Television Aesthetics and Style*, where James Zborowski writes, "If we think of aesthetics as being concerned with renewing perception and of studies of the everyday as being concerned with reclaiming experience, then it is not hard to see the connections between the two endeavors."[7] And in their introductory overview of the field of television studies, Jonathan Gray and Amanda D. Lotz assert that aesthetics, tied to critical analysis, is "a key frontier for the field."[8]

"The cinematic" is the aesthetic concept driving the argument in this book. I will leave the term undefined for the moment, since the entirety of chapter 1 is devoted to a detailed elaboration of the concept. But the charged and politicized arguments that still swirl around the phrase "cinematic television" must be addressed here, at the outset. My argument in the pages that follow will be that the phrase "cinematic television" has been used much too casually and with too little conceptual rigor. The result is that enthusiasts of the phrase claim that television has ("finally") achieved the aesthetic sophistication of the cinema, which then leads nay-sayers to charge that the enthusiasts never really understood television to begin with and are simply reviving an outmoded and elitist taste culture to celebrate what is, in the end, just another example (however well made) of serial television.[9] So let me be clear: by making the argument that *Breaking Bad* is cinematic (*and* televisual), I am decidedly not weighing in on whether we are in the midst of a new golden age of television; nor am I making claims about the fundamental nature of the television medium. I am simply saying that—given the large-scale shifts in television mentioned earlier, along with the specific needs of a network like AMC[10]—an opening appeared, and *Breaking Bad* took advantage of that opening in an aesthetically decisive way. My focus is on one aesthetic regime that has emerged in relation to this opening; the extent to which this regime manifests itself in the many dramatic series constituting the landscape of television today will remain here an open question.

Film scholar Kara Keeling—who has in her own work developed and mobilized a concept of the cinematic (one that differs somewhat from the concept I will develop here)—found the need early on in her study to address the problem of the extent to which a concept like the cinematic might be "subsuming things specific to other audiovisual media, such as television, under the rubric of *cinema*."[11] Her answer to this, with which I concur, is that cinematic images are distributed all across the landscape of modern life: the cinema might at one time have been the primary vehicle for the dissemination of these images, but that does not mean that other audiovisual media do not traffic in them. Following from this, I propose that we think of the cinematic as a kind of flickering across the audiovisual landscape. Here, I borrow from Jacques Lacan his notion that the unconscious functions via a kind of flickering that interrupts the smooth flow of the symbolic/imaginary narratives that construct our world of "common sense."[12] Lacan's intent here was to insist that the unconscious was not a deeply buried secret but instead was always there on the surface, if only we had the eyes to see it. So too, throughout the history of television, the cinematic has flickered—perhaps more or less brightly—and we can see it in Lucy Ricardo's channeling of the gestures of Charlie Chaplin as she negotiates what it means to be a housewife in 1950s America, or in Hitchcock's television series' defamiliarization of the new object world of a modernizing nation; in the sudden appearance of the cinema verité camerawork in the Grant Tinker procedurals; and in myriad other examples of decisive aesthetic moments in television.

Keeling's concept of the cinematic is extremely broad, so that the cinematic image becomes the principal mode for organizing perception and constructing notions of common sense; it is thus for her one of the central mechanisms for the reproduction of capitalist social relations. There are, for sure, cinematic images that open onto excess and thus have the potential to disrupt the oppressive narratives of common sense, and these are images that Keeling valorizes and looks for in the works she analyzes. The intellectual infrastructure organizing Keeling's entire project is formidable; nevertheless, in this study I want to argue for a more narrow conception of the cinematic. As will become clear in chapter 1, I argue that the cinematic should be seen as a kind of interruptor within the regime of images. When we talk about common sense, we are ultimately talking about narratives, however much they have been generated by images, and the organization of images always has the potential to introduce gaps, uncertainties, contradictions in the narrative of which they are a part. In this book, "the cinematic" will be the term I use to name these particular types of images. As such, it names the occurrence of *an aesthetic event*: one that opens onto the indeterminate, one that leaves us "without criteria" with which to assess its sense—or, indeed, its common sense.[13]

Before moving into a discussion about the uniqueness of *Breaking Bad* to an understanding of cinematic television, I must take up one very interesting line of argument about contemporary serial television. In this argument, there is a curious parallelism going on, in which the textual narrative, often centered on the vicissitudes of the beleaguered white American male, can be seen as a reflection of the battles of those lonely, courageous new showrunners—themselves of course white males as well—against the entrenched and conservative bureaucratic businessmen who run television in the postnetwork era. In other words, just as the showrunner—often well tutored in the works of neorealism, the European new waves, and the great American auteurs—must fight the philistines in order to produce television that is "cinematic," so too the new wave of antiheroes crowding the ether are battling the more invisible economic and social forces that have rendered the white middle-class family man, once a staple of prime-time television, more and more precarious. Yet another layer of complexity can be added to this picture when we consider the ways in which the cable networks themselves, at the narrative level, look to shows that will align with their "brand." For example, HBO can favor the entrepreneurial heroes of *The Sopranos* or *Six Feet Under* because those heroes stand in for HBO itself, as it historically saw itself as the little guy battling the entrenched networks, while it can pass on *Mad Men*, whose retro stylings then become the perfect expression of AMC's library of classic American films.[14] These lines of thinking lead us to engaging arguments about contemporary premium television—especially in relation to a neoliberal socioeconomic regime that is at once its condition of possibility and at the root of its narrative and thematic terrains.

In the case of *Breaking Bad*, these thematic and narrative connections to neoliberalism are almost too obvious to need recapitulating here. Extensively written about in the press and among fans, they constitute what everyone already knows about *Breaking Bad*. Cancer might just as well be a metaphor for the white middle-class male, here caught in the throes of midlife crisis, sexual inadequacy, ineffectuality, inability to provide for family, and "bad" life choices (and let's face it, within the logic of neoliberal self-fashioning and the entrepreneurial creation of one's "career trajectory," being a high school teacher must be seen more and more as something one is consigned to, after all one's "better options" have played out).[15] More than that, though: crystal meth, it has been argued, is the neoliberal drug par excellence, and the story of its wildfire spread across the American heartland is closely connected to the de-industrialization (and de-unionization) of vast swaths of this heartland, forcing an increasingly impoverished (and largely white) former middle class to work impossible hours for less money and no benefits. These conditions lay at the heart of the meth epidemic across the nation.[16] Meth was situated within a contradiction whereby on the one hand, it brought marginalized workers "up to speed," so to speak, with the impossible demands of the de-unionized job market, while at the same time, it physically and financially ravaged them.[17] As for the geopolitics of the meth trade, *Breaking Bad* seems attuned to the history here, in which the white biker gangs originally centrally involved in meth production and distribution were gradually displaced by the Mexican cartels. In *Breaking Bad*, of course, the cartels are the dominant players, but the neo-Nazis who appear in season five become something of a "return of the repressed," once Walter White destroys Gus Fring's drug empire.

Given all this, *Breaking Bad* seems particularly suited to the kinds of ideological and representational analyses that have grounded television studies from the beginning; and, in fact, the series has generated several scholarly collections that by and large follow these general approaches in understanding it.[18] Given television studies' foundational investment in feminism and the politics of identity, one can understand how this particular story—with its relentless focus on the beleaguered, angry, middle-aged white male, deceiving his wife, mowing down a host of ethnic others, and making alliance with neo-Nazi thugs—might present real stumbling blocks to its critical assessment. Indeed, the entire issue of the "difficult men" of contemporary quality television brings to mind Robert B. Ray's understanding of post-1960 developments in Hollywood's portrayal of American mythology, which he characterizes as being divided into "left" and "right" cycles.[19] In a nutshell, Ray argues that in a period (not unlike today) of both intense aesthetic innovation and deep political polarization, Hollywood genre filmmaking split into two cycles, based on the way each cycle handled its approach to American mythology. In today's television, *The Wire* would be the paradigmatic example of the left cycle in prestige series, and would any series be a better candidate for the right cycle than *Breaking Bad*?[20]

But here I would return more closely to Ray's argument: he notes that the two films that "complete" the cycles—*The Godfather* (Francis Ford Coppola, 1972) in the case of the left cycle and *Taxi Driver* (Martin Scorsese, 1976) in the case of the right—are both "critical" works in the sense that they expose the unspoken assumptions and implicit contradictions that drove the cycles to begin with. Now, both *The Godfather* and *Taxi Driver* are crucial intertexts in the series *Breaking Bad*. But rather than argue that *Breaking Bad* performs some kind of synthesis of the two tendencies, I would instead claim that it performs critical work on contemporary American mythology similar to that being done in the two films. And if it seems now a precondition of their cultural work that those two films were steeped in knowledge of cinema culture—both Coppola and Scorsese being among those "movie brats" of New Hollywood who were the first directors to come out of film schools—I will argue in the following chapters that it is precisely the cinematic that allows *Breaking Bad* to do its own critical work.

I am not the first commentator to create a binary opposition between *The Wire* and *Breaking Bad*. Notably, Jason Mittell has also done so, in relation to the idea of "narrative complexity" that he argues has characterized some dramatic television since the 1990s. Given how I've presented the concept of the cinematic so far—namely, as an interruptor of narrative logics—it may be no surprise that this study will be coming at *Breaking Bad*, and contemporary television more generally, from a completely different angle to Mittell's. But since his argument has achieved a certain degree of traction in television studies, I will lay out my objections. The first has to do with his argument that one of the main appeals of complex narrative concerns how such complexity keeps the audience focused on the pyrotechnics of the moves in the storytelling, awed by the twists and turns that have emerged from the writers' room. He calls this the "operational aesthetics" of complex television;[21] and while it may be true that audiences react this way, this kind of logic can never take us beyond audience response, toward the kinds of work the narrative details are doing beyond producing some kind of Pavlovian (or more complex) reaction. D. A. Miller is very clear on the limitations of technicist approaches to criticism in his wickedly funny analysis of the "hidden" cuts in Hitchcock's *Rope*, where the critics' relentless focus on technique obscured what was *really* going on with those simulated long takes, just as it kept at bay any consideration of what was *really* going on between Brandon and Phillip (and David? and Rupert? and . . .).[22]

My second objection has to do with how Mittell uses *The Wire* and *Breaking Bad* to construct an opposition between "vast" and "dense" seriality, with *The Wire*'s narrative moving outward in ever wider circles of the sociopolitical, and *Breaking Bad*'s narrative moving inward to ever deeper depths of interiority and backstory.[23] But can the "inner" and the "outer" really be separated so conveniently? In the case of *Breaking Bad,* this reifies a certain bourgeois conception of "psychology" in a series that in fact continually distances itself from such a conception. As I will argue, the cinematic in *Breaking Bad* makes any such division between interiority and exteriority problematic.

In the first single-authored scholarly work on *Breaking Bad,* Elliott Logan, after noting the same tendencies in the critical analysis of the series that I have just sketched out, argues that "such frameworks may actually somewhat inhibit more nuanced understandings of what is going on in *Breaking Bad* at the granular level of style through which the series' story is presented."[24] Logan aligns himself with a relatively recent strand of television criticism that attempts to understand how the repetitions, delays, and patterns within serial television create unique tensions between the part and the whole.[25] At the same time, he embraces a much older tradition within film studies which insists that the work itself be taken "on its own terms," that we come to understand the work through its own expressive unfolding.[26] This is a position I'm in general agreement with. What I find limiting in Logan's nonetheless elegant study—and where my work will differ from his—is the way everything that happens "at the granular level" (and here I would say, at the level of mise-en-scène) ends up getting enchained to the series' character development and narrative lines. This is what David Bordwell calls "the way Hollywood tells it": all of the expressive elements of the frame must exist in the service of telling the story, or else they are consigned to the realm of "excess."[27]

This view coincides with the American entertainment industry's own understanding of what it does, so that the primacy of story and character is a veritable mantra for Hollywood's creative class. But there is another tradition, at least as old as the surrealists, for engaging with the cinema. In this tradition—arguably at least partly shared by the practitioners of *photogénie*, Walter Benjamin, the *Cahiers* critics of the 1950s, assorted other champions of mise-en-scène, and recent work that engages with these traditions, such as Miriam Hansen's *Cinema and Experience*—the magic of the cinema comes from its ability to set forth new and unexpected relationships between bodies, spaces, and worlds, and in such a way as to reprogram the human sensorium.[28] In this view, character and narrative become subsidiary to the more fundamental operations of the filmic image, as is evident from the surrealist practice of strolling randomly into movie theaters to watch fifteen-minute snippets of films. In recent film studies, this line of approach to moving images has been taken up most notably in the trendy turn toward the concept of "affect," or—to put it simply—the distribution of forces and energies within the image.[29] Affect, which in the moving image is produced through formal aesthetic relations within and among images, has the potential to become that *interruptor* of narrative I have already claimed as the province of the cinematic. As philosopher Davide Panagia notes, narrative too often becomes "narratocracy," a kind of common sense that occludes real thought, and the aesthetic event is what potentially suspends these narratives of common sense and pushes them in unexpected directions.[30]

In this book I will argue that the achievement of *Breaking Bad* lies precisely here, in how it affectively reconfigures the elements of our lives and our world via its cinematic manipulation of the elements of image and sound. In chapter 1 I specify very clearly what I mean by "cinematic" and establish that cinematic expression is a rare achievement even in cinema. But, as will become clear in the subsequent chapters, it is precisely through this suspension of representational politics that we can uncover richer and more profound ways that *Breaking Bad* finds expressive forms for—and ultimately even allegorizes—everyday life under the regime of neoliberalism.

There is a way in which *Breaking Bad* is cannily aware that the "straight corridor" of narrative cause and effect is only a surface effect, that underneath we can see odd effects of resonance, actions-at-a-distance, and radical indeterminacy.[31] This is nowhere more evident than in its use of the teaser or cold opening, which is often talked about in relation to nonlinearity but—in light of my argument here—is better thought of as presenting us with virtualities, or "possible worlds," only some fraction of which will ever be actualized. Perhaps this is one of the ways in which *Breaking Bad* most exploits its televisual form: the extended form of serial television enables things to come back, but with variations, and at greater distances than the feature film allows. Vince Gilligan has talked about the "chemical reactions" governing the way the narrative unfolds, and clearly he sees that in the realms of the social and of inner life—and the field of affects that lies at their conjuncture—chemical reactions often leave behind an indeterminable surplus or residue.[32] This is the fly in the ointment of cause and effect that the series continually plays with.

And in fact, it is with the literal fly that we can see this most easily. The fly is a recurring motif in the series, and an entire episode (310, "Fly") is, famously, devoted to the attempt to kill a fly that has contaminated the lab.[33] It is telling that this is a "bottle episode"—concocted "on the fly," so to speak, to economize on an overbudget production season by setting an episode in one location—for a bottle episode has exactly this character of being a surplus or leftover, so that once again the series is thematizing its own formal procedures. After the teaser, early in the episode Walter is fretting about how the numbers don't add up, the meth yield is consistently a fraction lower than it should be, as if even within the mathematical certainties of chemical cause and effect, something will always remain mysteriously unaccountable. He calls this a "vestige." The fly then comes to stand in for this unaccountability, something that Walt must stamp out at all costs, for if there is one thing he cannot abide, it is the existence of this mysterious "nothing" that underlies and drives everything. Significantly, then, after Jesse drugs him with sleeping pills in an attempt to calm his obsession with the fly, Walt mentally revisits his random encounter with Jesse's girlfriend Jane's father shortly before he watched her die, and spins out an alternative possible universe: if only he had died before going out that night . . .

But here I want to focus on the return of the fly in the teaser to episode 508 ("Gliding over All"), which ends the first half of the final season. The teaser begins as a fly alights on a desk lamp, and the camera rack focuses back to a close-up of Walter staring at the fly. Walt sits at the desk of the Vamanos Pest Control company (which is the front for the new meth operation) in a state of depressed paralysis. Here we should recall that the previous episode (507, "Say My Name") ended with Walt shooting business partner Mike because of Mike's refusal to give up the names of the jailed henchmen Mike has been paying to stay silent and who are now under DEA pressure to "flip." But this shooting, far from being an assertion of power by Walt, is instead the result of a hysterical loss of control, and almost as soon as he shoots Mike in the stomach, he realizes he has made a mistake and could easily have gotten the names from his new partner, Lydia. In a sense, we could say that he finally uses the gun we saw in the very first episode of the series—the gun that Hank forced him to handle, that he was so inept and uncomfortable holding, and that came to signify all his weaknesses—but only to reveal to himself and the world that despite his violent rise to the top, he remains a fundamentally reactive person: small, petty, insecure, afraid. It is interesting that when Mike makes his way to the river to die, the mise-en-scène has strong resonances to the scene in Sam Peckinpah's *Pat Garrett and Billy the Kid* (1973) in which the mortally wounded Lemuel (Chill Wills) lies at the river bank with Mrs. Baker (Katy Jurado) looking on, as Bob Dylan's "Knockin' on Heaven's Door" plays on the soundtrack, so that Walter is additionally feminized by this intertextual association.

But (back to 508) when Todd—Walt's new young partner and rival to Jesse—comes to the office looking for Walt and discovers him immobilized before the fly, there ensues a series of striking shots in which Todd, standing in the doorway, looks at the back of this lone figure sitting in the distance slumped in a chair (fig. I.1). It is at this point that a savvy spectator might note that these shots curiously resonate with one of the most iconic moments in classical Hollywood cinema: the climax of *Psycho* (Alfred Hitchcock, 1960) when Lila Crane (Vera Miles) goes into the fruit cellar and sees from behind the body of "Mother" slumped in a chair in the distance (fig. I.2). At once, the opening shots with the fly take on an entirely new set of meanings, as we recall the scene in *Psycho* when Norman-Mother (now merged) contemplates the fly on her hand and resolves not to kill it, to show the world that "she wouldn't hurt a fly" (figs. I.3 and I.4). Once we see that *Psycho* has become the intertext governing the orchestration of the mise-en-scène in this opening scene, it then comes as no surprise that shortly after that, when Todd rouses Walt to get to the task at hand (the disposal of Mike's body), we then see them standing before the trunk of a car into which Mike's dead body has been stuffed, just as Norman Bates (Anthony Perkins) puts the body of Marion Crane (Janet Leigh) into a car trunk after the shower murder (figs. I.5 and I.6). This set of associations continues after the teaser and into the episode proper, where the first thing we see is an overhead shot of Walter in the shower, in a composition strikingly similar to an early shot of Marion Crane's famous shower in *Psycho* (figs. I.7 and I.8).

We will get soon enough to the question of how to interpret all this; but in fact, the resonances with *Psycho* don't end with those shots. The methodical preparations Walt and Todd make as they prepare to dissolve the body in hydrofluoric acid echo the methodical way Norman Bates cleans up after "Mother," and the hydrofluoric acid Todd removes from a cabinet comes to stand in for the quicksand that Norman uses to erase the crime. But then, to end this reprisal of *Psycho*, there is yet another, more direct shot repetition: during Walt's shower, the camera moves outside the shower to observe, in the background, Walt reaching out from behind the curtain for a towel, while prominently in the foreground, sitting atop the toilet tank, is the volume of *Leaves of Grass* given to him by Gale Boetticher and inscribed with a dedication that

I.1. Todd finds Walt in the Vamanos office

I.2. *Psycho* (Alfred Hitchcock, 1960): Lila finds "Mother" in the fruit cellar

I.3. Walt studies the fly (the flesh-toned smear in the background is Walt's face, which will take form in a rack focus)

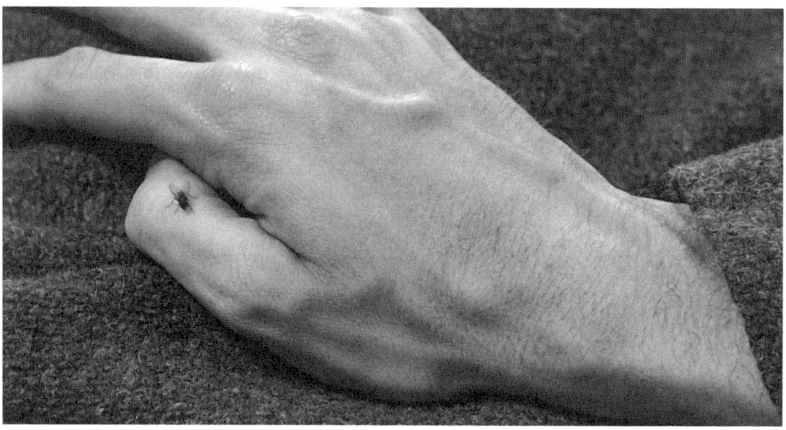

I.4. *Psycho*: Norman-Mother studies the fly

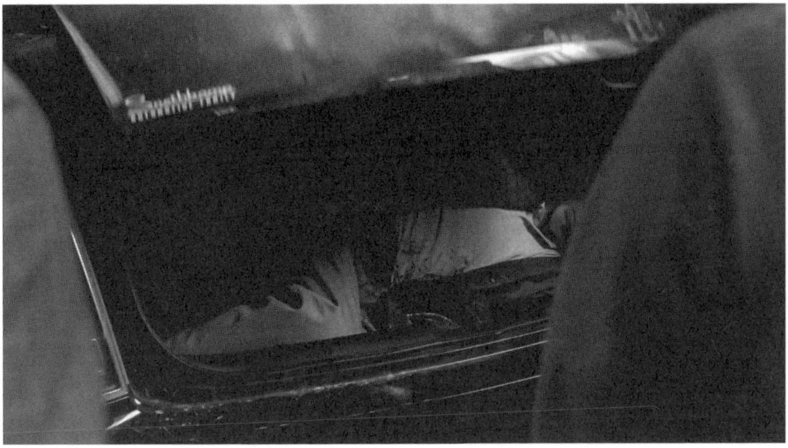

I.5. Disposing of the body

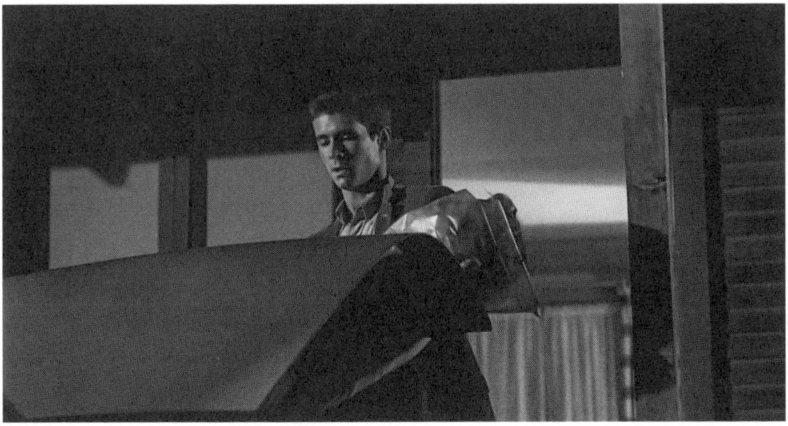

I.6. *Psycho*: Norman disposing of the body

1.7. *Psycho*: Marion's cleansing shower. Too late!

1.8. Walt's shower. Way too late?

could potentially expose Walt as the infamous drug kingpin Heisenberg (figs. I.9 and I.10). This resonates with two shots of the motel room in *Psycho*, in which Marion's newspaper is in the extreme foreground of the shot. In both cases, the foregrounded objects can potentially incriminate, but while Norman Bates finally notices the newspaper, Walter fails to see the Walt Whitman volume (and one can only think that some unconscious logic is making him not see that such a charged object is out of place).

It is important that we not take this extensive invocation of *Psycho* to be just another example of postmodern recycling. I would claim that there is nothing about the procedure here that smacks of pastiche or blank parody.[34] In a sense, this strategy (of which there are myriad examples throughout the series, some of them to be explored more deeply in the chapters that follow) is the formal equivalent of the fly itself: it gives the mise-en-scène a surplus (or remainder) that *keeps returning* in other guises. If what's happening at the granular level of mise-en-scène is a relentless pushing toward some Outside of narrative logic, then the repeated restaging of images from other films adds another, spectral dimension to the images. With all of these elements that cannot find their proper place, what psychoanalysis tells us is that such elements must keep returning. And so these hauntings within the images work alongside—and indeed as a constitutive element of—the mise-en-scène, to construct affective levels of possibilities within the images, to construct the possible worlds out of which the world of *Breaking Bad* is actualized.

This is why I don't think we need to muddy the waters with questions of intention at this point (chapters 1 and 2 address questions of the production system and its ethos in more detail). Certainly, we could come up with a number of explanations for why *Psycho* would be a critical intertext here. In episode 508, the series is looking toward its dark, final half season, and Hitchcock's *Psycho* is pervaded by a sense of things ending, not least of all classical Hollywood cinema itself. Then too there's *Psycho*'s dark vision of the American family, coming at a time when television—at least in the sitcoms—was constructing a phony and idealized image of the American family. But these "molar" or large-scale explanations keep returning us to the narrative of *Breaking Bad*, when the resonances with *Psycho* are happening at a granular level. At this level, we

I.9. The camera foregrounds incriminating evidence

I.10. *Psycho*: The camera foregrounds incriminating evidence

see Walter White being positioned alternately as Norman Bates, Marion Crane, and a stuffed dead corpse. It is as if, once the specter of *Psycho* begins to assert itself in the mise-en-scène, it cannot let go until all its associations play themselves out—failure of masculinity, failure of the nuclear family, failure of crime, failure of the American Dream.

This reading strategy does not mean that I will leave narrative and character considerations out of the picture. But in the interactions between form and narrative, I will attend at least as much to the tensions, contradictions, and leftovers or surpluses in this relationship as to the ways in which they are in accord. This, I wager, will deepen our understanding of the cultural work *Breaking Bad* is doing. Thus, to conclude this introduction, I think it would be useful to perform a mapping (via a semiotic square) of the cultural field *Breaking Bad* is situated within and working upon (fig. I.11). This should be taken as a preliminary starting point for the investigations to follow.

In this figure, the top axis—televisual family and ethnic enclave—is connected by an interrupted line. This reflects the historical fact that in early U.S. television, there is a move to repress the ethnic in situation comedies such as *The Goldbergs* and *Life with Luigi* and substitute for it the "white" middle-class family of the *Ozzie and Harriet* type. To a certain extent, despite all the morphings of the televisual family, this remains a central reference point in American television. At the two poles of opposition, we have the "Organization Man" and the loner/psychotic, both of which find all sorts of filmic and televisual representation. These compose the starting points of the semiotic field to be elaborated. In the case of *Breaking Bad*, Walter White moves across the line from the televisual family at the series' beginning to the psychotic at the series' end, while the ethnic enclave is seen largely through the Mexican drug cartel, and the Organization Man through Hank, the DEA, and the Madrigal corporation.

Things get more interesting when we look at the sublated terms in the square. Conspiracy, for example, which unites the Organization Man with the loner, is a strong part of Vince Gilligan's résumé from his work on *The X-Files* but is largely absent from *Breaking Bad*. We could say, though, that conspiracy's underlying psychic structures—paranoia, anality, and perhaps even homosexual panic—survive and attach them-

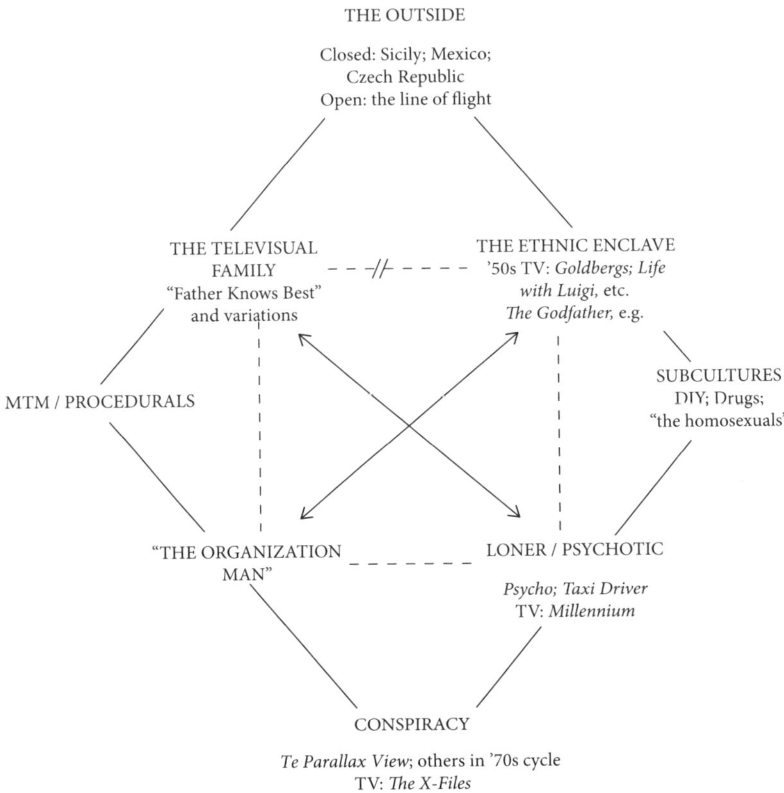

I.11. Semiotic square of the cultural field that *Breaking Bad* is situated within

selves to Walter White and other characters. (What might it mean that Walt consigns his enjoyment of Whitman—the poet who celebrated male-male love and "sang the body electric"—to those private moments when he is relaxing his anal sphincter?) So too the left-most term—the workplace as surrogate family—is largely absent in *Breaking Bad*, despite the scenes within the DEA offices. Instead, the workplace keeps invading the domestic spaces (and so begins to take on allegorical value as the nature of work continues to evolve in the U.S. economy).

By far the most interesting problems present themselves with the final two terms, what I am calling "the Outside" and "subcultures: 'the homosexuals.'" Subcultures names the place of minor knowledges and practices, the kinds of "do-it-yourself" cultures that are transmitted orally and remain outside official science. As such, this pole lies opposite that of the procedural (a staple genre of television). This is the world of drugs seen from the inside: the meth, for example, cooked up from books of matches and decongestant tablets. The reason I am emphasizing homosexuality here—and using what might be seen as old-fashioned terminology—has to do with how the series itself imagines the homosexual. In a certain way, it accords with the cultural demand—in force until only recently, and perhaps not entirely dead—for presenting homosexuality as "the open secret." It accords with the signifiers through which cultural production envisioned the homosexual, as member of an invisible "tribe," and as stigmatized and unhappy outsider to the reproductive fecundity of family. In other words, "the homosexuals" is presented here as a figure, and as queer theory has taught us, this figure is mobile and has the ability to attach itself to just about anyone.[35] This is how homosexuality is handled in *Breaking Bad*, and while it may seem politically retrograde in today's terms, it nevertheless may provide us with something of importance. Certainly, the character Gale Boetticher is queer. Gale is presented to us less as a unified, coherent person and more as an assemblage of disparate and incompatible traits: a Libertarian with *Fundamentals of Marxism-Leninism* on his bookshelf, a vegan, a chemistry geek, an afficionado of obscure Italian pop songs of the 1930s, a coffee perfectionist, and a hookah smoker. Together, these work to create a quirky, likeable character, although one senses with Gale that "there's no there there." But then isn't the support he received from his mentor Gus Fring a case of "gay tutelage"? This entire motif of the open secret is given expression by the circulating volume of Whitman's *Leaves of Grass*.

Within much popular cultural production, the Outside has been figured as that utopian "elsewhere" where the characters might finally achieve wholeness. Mexico is paradigmatic here: think, for example, of how Mexico functions as such in Nicholas Ray's *They Live by Night* (1948), in which the young lovers on the run see Mexico as the place where they can finally be free. Or we could consider the role Sicily plays in the first *Godfather*: it becomes the place where Michael can finally resolve his conflict between family and "America," where he achieves wholeness through his meeting of Apollonia (*nomen est omen*). But in *Breaking Bad*, Mexico is already enfolded into the ethnic enclave; it is as if, in Fredric Jameson's terms, the Outside no longer exists as a viable alternative to globalized capitalism, and instead we get the meth market in the Czech Republic, liberated from communism and now in the throes of drug consumption.

But the Outside can designate a more abstract elsewhere. Drugs, for example, might provide a line of flight from the present, though they are dangerously unreliable in that regard. However, aesthetic experience, insofar as it forces us to reinvent the coordinates through which we see the world, throws us outside of the common sense of everyday life. Here, then, is where *Breaking Bad* reflexively folds in on itself, such that we find the opening onto the Outside to lie deep within its haunted (and haunting) images.

As we move through this study and begin to look more closely at the cinematic archive that haunts the images of *Breaking Bad*, we will understand just how profound are the stakes of this procedure. For by and large, these haunted images harken back to films that were—in their critical orchestrations of the world—sounding alarms at the state of American culture. Today, television allows these disparately strewn alarm bells to ring week after week, now in the context of a present state of emergency. It shows us the ways in which our present is inextricably tied to these earlier cultural moments, even as it holds to the optimism that television might just be able to perform that reconfiguration of sensibility we have long hoped the cinema would bring to fruition.

1 The Cinematic

The notion that in the past decade or so, television—or more precisely, a certain kind of television—has become "cinematic" is as much a commonplace among industry workers, critics, and fans as it is a contentious point of debate for those engaged in academic television studies. If at the outset we can say one thing for certain about televisual cinematics, it is that the concept is highly overdetermined. To begin with what is most obvious, certainly technological innovations have provided a large percentage of the home viewing audience (within the relatively affluent nations, at least) greater real estate in the image, and a more distributed soundscape, which makes home viewing potentially more akin to film spectatorship than it had ever been before the spread of digital technologies. Industrial shifts in the postnetwork era—particularly shifts in the distribution and marketing of "product" toward smaller but more-targeted demographics, facilitated by the rise of pay cable and premium networks—allowed for the exploration of themes and the production of images that before, in the network era, would have been deemed inappropriate for broadcast television but were even then commonplace in the cinema. To this one must add refinements in digital recording and the widespread diffusion of web 2.0, which made it very easy to engage in time shifting, binge viewing, and other commonplaces of current television viewing practices. To be sure, none of this is news. But from the point of view of the discourses surrounding the cinematic, it is easy to see how these technological, industrial, and cultural developments might lead to the widespread colloquial adoption of the term by way of analogy: screen size, audio density, thematic content, provocative images, and viewing practices all seem to converge toward cinema. And it is this analogical use of the term that causes problems for many television scholars (as indeed it will, for different reasons, in my own arguments to come).

For one thing (television scholars will note), the new wave of "quality television" labeled "cinematic" in the postnetwork era is nevertheless embedded within older, inertial institutional structures that impose on these shows certain formal qualities that are eminently televisual: the narrative must be parsed out into episodes of a series, and within an episode the narrative must structure itself around a fixed number of commercial interruptions. Even those series made for pay cable and initially broadcast without commercial interruption are subject to this demand for programmed narrative pacing, insofar as the network underwriting the series has one eye on the market for syndication of the series after its initial run, a highly lucrative revenue stream. Thus, a certain kind of televisual rhythm is imposed on the unfolding narrative. In contemporary television, this is generally achieved by multiple story lines that intersect at various key points in the episode but that allow for a greater *combinatoire* when assembling (or reassembling) the episode to allow the commercial breaks to be inserted. Thus, there is at least one formal level—that of narrative construction—where the analogical appeal to the cinematic breaks down.

But cinematic television as a concept is also criticized at a more polemical and politicized level from within television studies. In this argument, to call television cinematic is to invoke a cultural hierarchy of distinction, in which the "good object" of cinema is appealed to in order to redeem television as a "debased object" mired in banality and bad taste. In other words, the appeal to the cinema reinvokes the high-low distinction that by necessity had to be challenged in order to establish television studies as a discipline in the first place. When HBO adopted its advertising slogan "It's Not TV, It's HBO," it was mobilizing this high-low distinction—the notion, at least among a certain demographic of viewers, that television was, if not a "vast wasteland," at least an unexciting sea of uniformity—in order to convince subscribers that they were paying for something that they could not get elsewhere free.[1] Clearly, this appeal to the empty signifier "not-television" (which generally ends up being filled in by some notion derived from the cinema) was a clever attempt at product differentiation by creating a paradox in which television ends up delivering itself from itself.

It is worth recalling that the current wave of quality television is not the first case in which the term "cinematic" has been used to describe aesthetic developments in television, and that in fact the appeal to the cinematic has been a recurring strategy in attempts to explain or understand stylistic innovations within the medium. Thus, for example, when the Steven Bochco/MTM series *Hill Street Blues* rethought the cops/procedural genre by—among other things—adopting handheld camerawork and other aesthetic strategies of verité, the series was seen as breaking long-standing televisual conventions in a cinematic way. Interestingly, in 1984, just a few years after the premiere of *Hill Street*, another police procedural with a completely different visual style, *Miami Vice*, was also described as cinematic, at the very same time that it styled itself after the quintessentially televisual form of the music videos then dominating the programming of MTV.[2] Certainly, "cinematic" was a capacious enough term to handle both of these styles: after all, there is a long-standing tradition in film studies that characterizes the cinema via two "tendencies" that can be traced back to the earliest work of the Lumière brothers and Georges Méliès, one tendency toward the documentary recording of everyday events and another toward the play of composition and montage. And in the case of *Miami Vice*, the sun-drenched pastels and deep blacks of its color palette were only possible through the use of the new Kodak 5290 line of ultrafast, fine-grained film stock.

It is in relation to the television production of the 1980s that John Caldwell developed the notion of "televisuality" to describe what he calls a major paradigm shift in how television presented itself: it moved, he argues, toward modes of presentation in which the television image, far from being the pared-down, stunted "delivery system" for narrative, dialogue, and information (as scholars like John Ellis had argued), instead became invested in all manner of stylistic excess or extravagance. Caldwell's concept has the advantage of not being tied to any specific look: televisuality can manifest itself in various forms, as it simply marks the fact that style is now exhibiting itself. For example, the development of digital effects and nonlinear video editing systems allowed for stylistic exhibitionism in the graphic elements of the television image—spinning logos, resizeable rectangles, and so forth—that were by and large confined to news broadcasting, some music video, and network branding. This contrasts with the stylistic exhibitionism of shows like *Hill Street* or *Miami Vice*, which relied on technologies and conventions from the cinema for the creation of surplus value in the images. Caldwell thus constructs a gradient in which the cinematic and the videographic lie at two poles of an axis, so that across the decade, one can position each series or television event at some point along this axis, with *Miami Vice* falling very far on the cinematic side, while an unfolding and partly live news story like that surrounding the Rodney King beating would fall very far on the videographic side.[3]

As useful as this schematic is for understanding television style in the 1980s, the nature of the term "cinematic" remains a problem. Caldwell's definition of the term is still analogical (if not tautological): "The cinematic refers, obviously, to a film look in television." He then notes that this means more than just shooting on film, since that practice dates back to the 1950s; it means the importation of other characteristics of the cinema, here singled out as "spectacle, high production values, and feature-style cinematography."[4] The problem here is that yet again, an analogical relation is being constructed around a set of arbitrarily chosen (and vaguely defined) features: in this particular case, the cinematic seems to emerge out of a kind of "self-positing," in which is reified a certain view of the cinema held by the industry and popular audiences. Certainly, it isn't difficult to come up with examples of films with low production values that one would call highly cinematic: much of classical Hollywood's B-picture output might be so described. But this suggests that there is another way to think of the term "cinematic," one that is less analogical than it is conceptual.

Historically, the term "cinematic" achieved critical traction in the 1960s (in the United States), in the heyday of auteurism and the construction of a film canon, and was closely connected to those two projects.[5] Perhaps the quickest way to illustrate the conceptual valences of the term—that is, what makes it more complex than the descriptive uses just outlined allow for—is to consider such claims as "Not all films are cinematic," or even more radically, "A large number of films made are not cinematic." These statements encapsulate very well the ethos surrounding the deployment of the term "cinematic" during the early institutionalization of film studies: no particular film is automatically cinematic; whether or not a film can be called cinematic is the result of an aesthetic judgment concerning how its images and sounds are recorded, manipulated, and organized. In other words, the cinematic had to do with the possibilities of the medium, with what the cinema could, potentially, do.

At a time when film studies was still struggling for a place in the university curriculum, the concept of the cinematic served to specify an object and a method of study: instead of reducing film to a "simple" medium of visual translation for art that already existed in literary or dramatic form—a position that legitimated film only insofar as it performed adaptations of the art of "dead white males"—one needed to attend methodologically to the specific ways the images were constructed and orchestrated, to the film's mise-en-scène and editing, in order to understand what the film was doing and to assess its aesthetic value. Thus, the cinematic worked precisely to overturn the cultural hierarchies and high-low distinctions of an institutional elite,[6] insofar as it allowed us to valorize a popular film adapted from a pulp novel over and above a pedestrian adaptation of a Shakespeare play, for example.

It is thus something of an irony that when the cinematic migrates to television, it is criticized for being hopelessly enmeshed in the taste culture of an elite. On one level, this might be seen as a sign of the successful integration of film studies into the academic institution, so that whereas film studies fought against the entrenched taste cultures established by literature departments, television studies had to stake its claim to legitimacy largely from within established film departments. This is to adopt a familiar "oedipal narrative" to explain historical change.[7] On another level, though, there is a dissymmetry involved in the narratives of the establishment of the two disciplines. While film studies rejected the categories through which literary studies understood film texts and replaced them with others—like mise-en-scène and editing—more suitable to the objects of study, it didn't (yet) abandon aesthetics as the fundamental framework through which to understand its objects. Because of the nature of television—that is, as "technology and cultural form," to use Raymond Williams's phrase—television studies had to seek its methodological discourses from the emerging field of cultural studies, where aesthetic judgments tended to be bracketed out.[8]

That cultural studies has generally had trouble with questions of the aesthetic is not news.[9] But from the point of view of debates surrounding the legitimacy of the term "cinematic" when applied to television, the solution to the problem will hinge on whether, and to what extent, aesthetic judgment can find a place within television studies. What would such an aesthetics look like? And could it be something that is not a "throwback" but rather that genuinely builds on and adds to the already rich tradition of television studies? The wager of this book is that "the cinematic" as an aesthetic concept will allow us to answer these questions. As I explained in the introduction, my conception of the cinematic has much in common with the way Kara Keeling develops the term—through a reading of Gilles Deleuze—in her book *The Witch's Flight*. Insofar as we see the cinematic as a kind of relay between "a complicated aggregate of capitalist social relations, sensory-motor arrangements, and cognitive processes" accomplished through the manipulation and arrangement of images, there is no reason to insist that such image relays can exist *only* in the cinema.[10] In relation to *Breaking Bad*—and to contemporary serial television more generally—we can simply note that dramatic changes in technology and industrial norms have given these images increased importance.

But there remains one obstacle to be cleared away before the argument can move forward: the notion of the auteur, which is, historically, inextricably connected to the development of the term "cinematic."[11] Methodologically, the cinematic required us to look to visual organization in order to understand the cinema. But as recurring patterns of visual organization were discovered, these stylistic traits became associated with the name of an auteur, became marks of an authorial "signature." Alfred Hitchcock, for example, orchestrates the system of looks (via framing, editing, camera movement) in such a way as to produce an uneven distribution of knowledge among the various characters and the spectator. Not only does this create Hitchcock's trademark suspense, but it also produces a cinematic world in which every action is potentially deceptive or revelatory and thus must always be interpreted. This move toward infinite interpretation ("terminable or interminable") is what aligns Hitchcock's work so neatly with psychoanalysis as a practice or, indeed, with the espionage narratives to which Hitchcock was so drawn.

What is important to note in this procedure—and what is sometimes misunderstood—is that one does not begin with the thematic material in reconstructing the world of any given auteur: thematic material arises insofar as it is an *expression* of a visual style. This is the only way we can resolve what might seem like a fatal contradiction at the heart of the auteur policy,[12] which becomes apparent whenever a director's work is characterized at the outset by the thematic materials she or he favors. For clearly, narrative structures and genre conventions can be central to the creation of thematic material, and these are arguably outside the agency of the director (or at the very least arrived at collectively among key creative personnel). But it is not far-fetched to presume that the film director at least has the potential to be in charge of the elements of the visual organization of the shots.

A similar problem arises from the other direction, if you will, at the level of visual style, when one considers that at any given time, a particular set of best practices is upheld within the various crafts that make up the industry; these practices can thus be seen as the underpinning for what David Bordwell identifies as the "norms" of the system.[13] It is only when directors push against or orchestrate these norms in creative and meaningful ways that they achieve the status of auteurs; and it is only insofar as the resulting style is expressive of ideas that we can then talk about the thematic preoccupations of the various auteurs, or of the "worlds" that they create. Given all this, the term "cinematic" is less a designation of medium specificity than it is a fundamentally aesthetic judgment about newness or originality against the backdrop of the conventionality endemic to mass-produced art.

It might be argued that none of the above can hold traction when one is thinking about television, insofar as its mode of production is so different. The "product" is not a discrete, self-contained, time-limited work but a series, often of indeterminate duration. Whereas in film, the script can be the anchor for directorial exploration, in the television series the story line is not fixed in advance, but evolves in group meetings among the series' writers; the quick production schedules of television require that such elements of mise-en-scène as lighting schemes and sets be developed by creative teams for the series as a whole (much as the studios of Hollywood's classical era developed house styles for lighting, etc.). This means that it is more often the producer (or, in the postnetwork era, the showrunner) who is thought of as the key figure behind the television series, with the direction of individual episodes being assigned to a whole roster of directors. But my earlier discussion of the cinematic shows that—for many film scholars, at least—the auteur has become more than anything a heuristic device for categorizing the many ways in which the cinema has in its history orchestrated bodies in space (which is one quick and simple way to define mise-en-scène). Thus, we value the 1950s melodramas of Nicholas Ray because of the ways in which they orchestrate bodies and their actions within the spatial regimes of the new suburban housing developments, regardless of what intentions Ray may have had as director of the films. "Mise-en-scène," then, is the term that describes the potentially infinite ways that the cinematic manifests itself; the criteria by which we assess the success or failure of a particular film has to do with whether its orchestration of bodies and spaces opens up new avenues for seeing our world. Thus, to talk about cinematic television is to talk about mise-en-scène and not about authorship, in precisely the ways sketched out here.

As I've noted, mise-en-scène criticism connected to auteurism in the 1960s worked to overturn a cultural hierarchy by arguing that it was largely lower-budget productions that produced the most interesting mise-en-scène.[14] It's not hard to provide possible explanations for this: low-budget productions have less investment at risk and will thus tend to be less supervised by the studio hierarchy; one could even argue that the quick production schedules of low-budget films encouraged more improvisation in lighting, camerawork, and staging. Interestingly, Vince Gilligan in a television interview used an analogous argument to make the case that today, the most creative work is likely to be found on television rather than on the movie screens. He noted that the extremely high capital investment required for feature filmmaking in the United

States today results in such a slowed-down process from concept to execution that it drains the production of the initial flush of creative energy that motivated it.[15]

In this sense, we could say that today's quality television stands in the same relation to popular feature filmmaking as the low-budget auteurist cinema of the 1950s stood in relation to Hollywood's A-list productions. It should come as no surprise, then, that *Breaking Bad* abounds in influences not just from the 1950s auteurist tradition but from low-budget cinemas of mise-en-scène ranging from spaghetti westerns to *The Godfather*. (*The Godfather* was never imagined by Paramount to be the sensation that it turned out to be, and its original budget was about 20 percent of that of an A-list picture).[16] But rather than examples of postmodern recycling or blank parody, the series' extensive borrowings from the cinematic canon seem to be attempts at thinking through what a television of mise-en-scène might look like; in addition, they allow the series to situate its own unique presentation of the bodies and spaces of the twenty-first century within a larger tradition of mise-en-scène that was highly critical of postwar American exceptionalism and affirmative culture. The series thus is able to nod to this tradition while bringing it forward into new social spaces, technologies, and lifeworlds.

As it happens, mise-en-scène has recently made something of a comeback in film studies. For example, Adrian Martin's book on the subject, *Mise en Scène and Film Style*, presents a nuanced history of the term as it has evolved in film studies and gives us a sense of the complexities and even contradictions encompassed in the concept. For my purposes, I'd like to take one idea from Martin's reading of the mise-en-scène of David Cronenberg's *History of Violence* (2005) and use it to develop a concept of mise-en-scène that I believe will be "synoptic," resolving some of the concept's problematic implications while at the same time being particularly suitable to understanding cinematic television. In what is a rather conventional reading of the Cronenberg film—conventional in the sense that he is working from the assumption of a single work unified around certain stylistic and thematic resonances—Martin notes an early use of a doorway that recalls the famous door frame early in John Ford's *The Searchers* (1956); from this, he argues that the Cronenberg film will be an investigation into thresholds:

between civilization and wilderness, between crime and the Law, and so forth. In this way, the organization of the "raw materials" in the image comes to serve a unifying thematic purpose in keeping with both the western generic tradition and the specific ways it has been inflected by past auteurs like John Ford.[17]

But in doing this, Martin has—perhaps inadvertently—hit on what I would argue is not simply a particularly apt instance of mise-en-scène, but one of its most fundamental properties. For the threshold presents us with an intensive relationship in the mise-en-scène. When we talk about crossing a threshold, we are referring not to the extensive movement of a body through space, but rather to the crossing of a certain limit point. For example, a body of water remains water even when energy is applied to it or removed from it, until it reaches a certain threshold or limit—a boiling point or a freezing point—after which the body of water fundamentally changes form. What I would like to propose here is that we think of moving-image texts such that the narratives provide us with *extensive* relations—movements and actions that produce those cause-effect chains that drive narratives forward—whereas mise-en-scène, insofar as it is effective, generally presents us with (the ability to see) *intensive* relations, the (virtual) "spaces in between" the causes and the effects, imparting to the narrative a sense of openness or possibility. In a certain sense, intensive relations transect the more linear relations formed by narrative, so that mise-en-scène will produce its effects via resonances, actions-at-a-distance, and so forth.[18] This perhaps explains why mise-en-scène analysis remains the province of a relatively small group of cineastes, while most discussions of films and television among fans and casual viewers focus largely on the narrative lines, ever careful to avoid "spoilers," and treat visual elements as decorative rather than functional.

In order to see how mise-en-scène as intensive relations actually works, we might look at a film like Nicholas Ray's *Bigger Than Life* (1956; not a random choice in relation to the series *Breaking Bad*). In this film, mild-mannered and financially strapped schoolteacher Ed Avery (James Mason) is stricken by a rare disease for which he must take the new miracle drug cortisone, which, unbeknownst to anyone, has potential side effects ranging from severe mood swings to outright psychotic breaks. The drug sets in motion in Avery a process of becoming-other, and he moves through a series of passages in which his psychotic megalomania jumps to ever higher levels. When—or perhaps better, how—will the drug kick in? How does the mise-en-scène then register this succession of intensive jumps?

About halfway through the film, Avery is preening before the medicine cabinet mirror while his wife lugs kettles of heated water upstairs to prepare his bath (as the water heater is ineffective). When his wife walks in with two more kettles, he opens the medicine cabinet to hide his narcissistic fantasies from her. But is the bath water hot enough? "One more kettle will do," Avery casually says to his wife, at which point she explodes, races toward him, and slams the medicine cabinet door shut, shattering the mirror. Later, concerned that their eleven-year-old son is behind in his mathematics, Avery suspends the family dinner and sequesters the boy in his study until he can solve a problem (itself a problem of intensity: if A can do a job in six hours and B in five hours, how quickly can the job get done with both working?). When Avery leaves the room for a minute, the mother sneaks into the study to give the boy a glass of milk. Later, with the family gathered at the dinner table, we notice on the milk pitcher the residue rings from the milk that has been poured out earlier. When Avery discovers his wife has "undermined" his pedagogical program for the boy, his paranoiac delirium moves to yet a higher level as he proclaims that their marriage is finished.

Of course, this latter scene could be put into the extensive series of causes and effects that constitute the narrative. But the mise-en-scène orchestrates the bodies and movements in such a way that the pitcher of milk becomes a kind of intensive relay for the flows of forces that traverse the space. At the film's climax, when this intensification process reaches its peak, Avery's patriarchal terror finds its originary myth in the sacrifice of Abraham, but all modulated through the charged objects of a football, a Bible, and a pair of scissors. Finally, with the television blaring insipid carnival music through the house, Avery's neighbor subdues Avery in a fight in which they both break through the bannister of the stairway that separates the intimate spaces of the upstairs with the more public facade that the ground floor presents to the world.

As has perhaps become evident from this description, *Breaking Bad*—

especially in its pilot, but also repeatedly thereafter in resonating images that flicker through the series—sets itself up almost as a remake (or rethinking) of *Bigger Than Life*: the schoolteacher has shifted from grade school to high school, the disease from "rare arterial inflammation" to lung cancer, the moonlighting job from cab dispatcher to car wash cashier. Both families live in modest, middle-class bungalows, where in both cases a failing water heater signals the patriarch's inability to provide the family with the most basic necessities. And the effects of drugs on the two teachers is to push them to higher and higher states of megalomania. While this echo of *Bigger Than Life* is only one of what will become many borrowings from the classical film canon in *Breaking Bad*, the Ray film can be thought of as the "primal" intertext of the series in that the very narrative premises and inciting situations are parallel. But this borrowing—like the many others throughout the series—is, as I've already insisted, far from the "blank" citationality of much postmodern television; rather than being arbitrary and seemingly random eruptions from the image archive, the borrowings in *Breaking Bad* are sustained in such a way as to allow the thought expressed in the original to play itself out in a new context. This is why I use the term "borrowing" instead of the more usual "citation" to refer to these—because the borrowing starts with a mise-en-scène idea that is then carried through to its logical conclusion.

"Breaking bad"—the phenomenon that gives the series its title—is itself a term that indexes an intensive series of changes. It is about passing through certain thresholds. Vince Gilligan and members of the cast have talked in interviews about where to locate the mysterious point at which Walter White breaks bad.[19] This, however, refers the question back to narrative: back, in other words, to the reigning paradigm—embraced by the industry, critics, and fans alike—which mandates that all expressive devices be mobilized in the service of telling the story. But I would contend that the breaking bad from which the series derives its title points to no specific character but rather highlights a process, or a passage, that can range across all the various narrative permutations and thus becomes something like a modulator of the constantly shifting relations among bodies, objects, and spaces as the narrative moves forward. In other words, the series title announces its affinity to mise-en-scène (as I have characterized it above). This, then, gives us our first clue as to why Gilligan may have thought to inaugurate the series via an extended reworking of a film that not only is celebrated for its mastery of mise-en-scène but also is the work of a director who was central to the early elaborations of the concept of the cinematic.

For these reasons, *Breaking Bad* can not just be seen as the paradigmatic example of the most recent wave of cinematic television; much more importantly, it allows us to see how contemporary cinematic television differs from all of its previous instantiations. No doubt this is deeply connected to the technological shifts that have added greatly increased screen real estate and definition in home viewing: one of the corollaries of our understanding of mise-en-scène as an achieved orchestration of intensities (as opposed to being simply a look) is that it clearly requires greater space for seeing minute interrelationships between elements of the image. In a sense, this is the condition of possibility for the opening up of televisual language to the mise-en-scène traditions of classical and postclassical cinema.

On another level, though, the American mise-en-scène tradition that flourished from the 1940s through to the New Hollywood of the 1970s was a critical one: more often than not, the intensities produced within these films pushed against the certainties of official national discourses, precisely by tracking the instabilities lurking behind the structures of everyday life.[20] Thus, for example, Nicholas Ray's cinemascope films of the 1950s—including *Bigger Than Life*—use all the resources of the cinemascope aspect ratio to visualize the suburban tract house cracking under its own weight. This is key: mise-en-scène is not imposed on the material from the transcendental position of the auteur wanting to make a statement about postwar suburbia, but rather is the immanent unfolding of the logic of the space, "coaxed" from the world by (in the case of Ray) directorial attention. Given *Breaking Bad*'s extensive immersion in this archive of mise-en-scène, the question that must animate the rest of this study is, What are the aesthetic and political implications of this move?

Before moving on, a word needs to be said about this book's understanding of textuality and its relationship to authorial intention. In the commentary track for the pilot episode, Vince Gilligan forcefully repudiated any auteurist notion that the series was governed by the artistic vision of any one person, describing instead a model of collaborative work that is, in fact, the official discourse of mainstream Hollywood (and has become a mantra during Academy Awards ceremonies).[21] I agree with Gilligan on this point, even if I approach this issue from a different angle: namely, from the angle of "the death of the author," which has come to be articulated in the theoretical humanities since the late 1960s. But what then allows us to attribute aesthetic value to consistencies in mise-en-scène across the series episodes, let alone to the wide-ranging visual references to the traditions of American auteurist cinema?

Here it is crucial to see that what underwrites aesthetic judgment after "the death of the author"—what allows us to analyze texts—is the idea that no single text can be seen as self-contained or autonomous, but each is rather a "node" in the vast intertextual network of signs, conventions, genres, tropes, and so forth, which constitute the very conditions out of which the single text can make any sense. This extends to the vast archive of images that has only proliferated in the age of web 2.0. Every new image (or every new instance of mise-en-scène) exists against the backdrop of this global "virtual" image archive—virtual in the sense that images not only circulate through the ether of global information flows but also are distributed in varying degrees as memory traces in the global consumer of images. (What reader cannot now conjure up an image of Marion Crane getting stabbed to death in the shower?) In addition, media practitioners—those engaged in the production of moving-image works—are more likely than not to have these traces of images readily available to them, if only because they have had to apprentice themselves to how moving images are put together. Given all this, it's clear that we need not search for any author single-mindedly creating images: we need only assume that the production team as a whole was attuned to this archive of images, and that *it was part of the ethos of the series* to develop these resonances and echoes. Thus, for example, the appearance of a fly in an episode must have triggered among the writers and production crew—as it certainly does among astute viewers of the series—a chain of cinematic memory images, from the fly buzzing around the hired gun at the beginning of Sergio Leone's *Once upon a Time in the West* (1968) to the fly buzzing around the cadaverous Norman Bates at the end of *Psycho.*

In contemporary theories of the image, there is a line of thought that argues that images have a life of their own.[22] A moving image glows from the LCD screen, and an image is actualized in our mind. Insofar as the image connects seamlessly with our sense of the world's order, it aligns with what Kara Keeling calls our common sense (with all the attendant potential tyrannies that can result). But these images contain an intensive force that at any moment can interrupt the homeostasis of common sense—this is what I am calling here the cinematic. In *Bigger Than Life,* the football and the sports trophy are enshrined on the mantel of the suburban home. But they move through a succession of charged meanings, until—caught up in the father's delirium—they signify a patriarchal terror that literally destroys the house from within.

Quoting Gilbert Simondon, Pasi Väliaho notes that the image "resists free will, refuses to let itself be directed by the will of the subject, and presents itself according to *its own proper forces*, inhabiting consciousness like an intruder who comes to upset the order of a house he was not invited to."[23] It is especially in the last phrase, in the suggestion of a home invasion, that Simondon's idea becomes most resonant to the idea of televisual cinematics. Of course, we invite television into our homes, and for the most part television obliges us with a certain amiability. But when the images become unruly, suddenly the memory traces of an entire archive—an archive of mise-en-scène—become active and available for use.

Mise-en-Scène and Narrative Causality

In order to differentiate mise-en-scène from set design, let's consider the drug deal with Tuco Salamanca in the auto graveyard, which ends season one (107, "A No-Rough-Stuff-Type Deal") and which is reprised and extended in the first act of episode 201 ("Seven Thirty-Seven"). In a panoramic establishing shot, we can see that the predominant design element is the strategic placement of red cars at key positions in the frame, which serve both to anchor the space and to guide the eye through various planes of depth. Of course, in retrospect, we might sense that the splotches of red that punctuate the graveyard anticipate the bloodiness unleashed by Tuco, which will similarly manifest itself in splotches and pools scattered through the space. But the location is also fraught with associational meanings: a DIY car culture that was once associated more generally with working-class American males but that now—outmoded in the context of white male leisure culture that has shifted toward informatics and digital culture more generally—has been taken up by Latino immigrants, whose often precarious status places them in the informal back-alley automotive repair economy. (The extent to which this DIY car culture among Latinos is driven by uneven economic development in the hemisphere is an interesting question, but certainly, the U.S. embargo of Cuba has made that culture a necessity there.) It is thus ironic when we find out that it is Walt who picked the location, and that not only does Jesse find the choice bizarre and dangerous, but Jesse's judgment is seconded by Tuco, who says, "What are we doing way the hell out here? What, they close the mall or something?" But at this point in the story, we are immersed in Walt's earliest experiences with the do-it-yourself culture of meth production, so it's as if the environment has set up an echoing circuit of exchange between the newly minted meth cook and his new wholesale buyer.

Jesse chides Walt that his choice of location was probably based on something he saw in the movies, which activates yet another associative chain, this time to the auto graveyard as iconic backdrop to the filmic presentation of the underside of the economic miracles of the 1950s and 1960s. This was the period when "fast cars, clean bodies" became the central focal point for the national modernization projects of the advanced capitalist economies; significantly, television played a central role in the dissemination and administration of these new desires for mobility and personal hygiene.[24] The auto graveyard thus became an iconic representation of "the repressed": at once a testimony to waste and unsustainability and an evocation of the terrible beauty of the outmoded, the neglected space that opened onto possibilities of escaping the implacable administration of everyday life via "tinkering" or other, more criminal pursuits. (The fantasy of a "perfect" cycle of production-consumption, with no waste or remainder, is a central idea that haunts *Breaking Bad* as a series.)

No filmmaker understood this more than radical French New Wave director Jean-Luc Godard, whose film *Sympathy for the Devil* (1968) juxtaposes a recording session of the Rolling Stones with scenes of black militants coming to political consciousness against the backdrop of an auto graveyard. Indeed, this seems to come as a sequel to his apocalyptic satire *Weekend* (1967), which is loosely structured around a weekend road trip and features a one-reel-long tracking shot of a traffic jam, followed by more and more flaming roadside car wreckage as the film moves toward neo-tribalism and cannibalism as the culmination of contemporary consumer culture. What Godard was on to—and what remains particularly relevant to any discussion of *Breaking Bad*—is how consumer culture erodes social linkages in such a way that everyday life becomes a scene of generalized warfare.[25]

Certainly, all of these associative connections add to the richness of our experience of these scenes. But to understand how all of this is mobilized as mise-en-scène requires us to attend to some very specific details in the image: most notably, the way the stacked cars introduce an instability between horizontal and vertical, so that something always seems to be on the verge of toppling over. When we first see the auto graveyard in episode 107, we cannot help but notice the way the cars are stacked on an angle; while they are no doubt in a stable arrangement, their weight seems to lean to the right, giving the impression that one slight move of one of the pieces might cause the entire wall of cars to come crashing down (fig. 1.1). Ultimately, cars *will* come crashing down in an offscreen event of which we see only the aftermath, but initially the instabilities in the mise-en-scène become actualized through the acts of an insane Tuco. After the deal between Walt and Tuco is made for weekly delivery of meth, one of Tuco's two henchmen, No-Doze, says to Walt, "Just remember who you're working for." This unsolicited warning from one of his lackeys sets Tuco off: at first he begins questioning No-Doze about his comment in a way that suggests the aggressive, sociopathic put-ons to which Tommy DeVito (Joe Pesci) in *Goodfellas* (Martin Scorsese, 1990) likes to subject his friends; then suddenly, and without warning, Tuco pummels No-Doze with punches until No-Doze loses consciousness and, as we discover in episode 201, ultimately dies before Tuco's car gets out of the graveyard. What we see here is a trans-

1.1. Instabilities in horizontal and vertical axes

ference, or a relay, in which the latent energies in the background get realized in the bodies of the characters. Equally important, the scene develops a central motif of the series, namely, the incommensurability between cause and effect. This is set up right from the beginning with the appearance of the nonsmoker Walt's lung cancer and is overtly thematized when Walt adopts the street name "Heisenberg."

Later in episode 201, a high stack of cars will end up killing Tuco's other henchman, Gonzo, as he tries to move the dead body of No-Doze, which was left in the auto graveyard. This happens offscreen; we only see the results when the police discover the bodies. According to the Blu-ray commentary, the tall stack of cars under which No-Doze's body is placed had to be carefully rigged in such a way that it could sway while at the same time being safe for the cast and crew working around it.[26] This confirms that mise-en-scène is something that is *achieved*: the unstable sense of grounding introduced early on is here extended via a technical device and a camera angle that—by enabling the stack of cars to sway—heightens our sense of precarity. And this is precisely what I mean by the intensive quality of mise-en-scène: the instabilities in the surroundings are strictly speaking virtual, until a threshold is passed and something—an event—materializes.

Recent film theory has approached this view of cinematic spectatorship through ideas of affect.[27] Affect is simply the variable distribution of forces among bodies in a space (i.e., a virtual force field); cinema, like other moving-image forms, is particularly suited to the presentation of affect, since each shot has the potential to register and reframe the constantly shifting forces in a particular environment (as in the auto graveyard example). One consequence of a shift of attention toward affect in the image is a lessening of attention to the narrative function of the images. This idea will require a bit of unpacking, but it is important first to clarify that the move toward affect in no way denies that the unfolding images have narrative value: anyone who looks at a picture of the writers' room of *Breaking Bad* (or any other contemporary television series) will see the dozens and dozens of note cards that carefully elaborate every turn of the plot for any given episode. And indeed, it is story line and character development that keep audiences and fans mesmerized by the series. Yet the notion of the cinematic automatically asks us to bracket out the narrative function of images, in order to look for something else.

Perhaps the best recent articulation of this view of cinema is by Jacques Rancière in his short book on the Hungarian director Bela Tarr. For Rancière, to look at an image—or a view on the world—solely in terms of its narrative function is to reduce the inherent complexity of the image (or of the world); we take what we need in order to understand the story, but we screen out or ignore all those elements of the image that are irrelevant (or only incidental, or excessive) to the unfolding narrative.[28] In other words, we instrumentalize, and thus oversimplify, the world around us. The image becomes just another link in the cause-effect chain that composes narrative. But in the films of Bela Tarr, Rancière notices an approach to the image that allows the forces inhering in the image—in other words, the affective dimension of the image—the time to unfold on their own. And while he doesn't say this, it could be argued that this is in fact the precondition for narrative to happen at all: something must be transmitted from one thing to another in order for a movement to occur, or for a thought to express itself in an action.[29]

One might object here that Rancière is discussing the work of one of the most rigorous and uncompromising auteurs of the art cinema, and that the dead time, the waiting, the de-dramatization of action that are all characteristics of the art cinema represent an aesthetic that is the polar opposite of that of any television series—even contemporary quality television—striving to capture even a small, cult following, let alone a mass audience. Now, it is true that *Breaking Bad* has adapted some of these aesthetic strategies for television, as have some of its predecessor series.[30] Certainly it exploits periods of waiting and dead time (as, for instance, in the scene in 407 when Walter, rather than return to the dealer—because of his wife Skyler's safety objections—the snappy Dodge Challenger he has bought his son, Walter Jr., for his sixteenth birthday, instead takes it for a joyride in a deserted parking lot and then lights a fire at the gas cap, casually walks away from the car, sits down, and telephones for a taxi, with the smoldering car in the background, waiting to explode). And it routinely slows down the "beats" within the episodes to allow for key scenes to play out for periods as long as ten to thirteen minutes; it even devotes entire episodes (e.g., 310, "Fly") to the elaboration of a seemingly trivial incident in a very confined space. Still, this extension of temporality is almost invariably linked back to the strong narrative lines that the series is constructing.

But while Rancière is talking about strategies of art cinema, this same veering of attention away from narrative function and toward affective relations within the frame was, for the postwar French critics mentioned earlier, the key strategy for understanding postwar American cinema in a new, auteurist light. True, the art cinema, by de-emphasizing narrative drive, makes it easier for us to discern how the forces within the image (and within the world) allow new things to emerge; but the French—and later American—commentators on postwar American cinema adopted this same procedure in viewing the Hollywood film. Suspend the attention to narrative elements of the visual field, and suddenly we are able to see the very particular universes that are being created by Nicholas Ray, Orson Welles, or Alfred Hitchcock, because we are taking an expansive view of mise-en-scène, one that goes beyond simple service to narrative cause and effect.

Rancière distinguishes these two ways of seeing as relative and absolute: relative ways of seeing reduce the visual world to so many links in a narrative, while absolute ways of seeing allow the latent forces accumulated in the bodies to unfold in their own ways and times, and as such introduce a breach, or a gap, within the narrative economy. And, at least in the case of Bela Tarr, whose cinema sets itself up in relation to the bureaucracies of state socialism (and, later, their sudden disappearance with the fall of the Eastern bloc), there is a strong political dimension to these ways of seeing the world. As Rancière puts it, "In order to exploit the breach offered, it is already necessary to loosen the constraint that binds the arguments of stories to the exposition of 'problems,' the existence and domain of which are defined by the powers of the planners."[31]

In *Breaking Bad*, this loosening runs through the entire series, starting with "the drug problem" itself, which is never seen in the simplistic and moralistic terms in which both official discourse and (its flipside) personal addiction narratives traffic. In the teaser to episode 107, for example, after the school janitor has been falsely accused of the theft of chemistry equipment and found to have had marijuana in his car, the insipidity of the parental outrage that ensues is underscored when Walter begins feeling Skyler up under the table; as the parental mass hysteria rises and Skyler becomes more sexually aroused, the voices in the room become more and more muffled—making all the discourses about "saving our children" seem increasingly clichéd—until the Whites' sexual reverie is interrupted by the sound of the principal calling out Walt's name. But the fact that parents are deluded about their children's relationship to drugs has already been established: in episodes 102 ("Cat's in the Bag . . .") and 103 (". . . And the Bag's in the River"), when Skyler's sister, Marie, stupidly assumes Walt Jr. is smoking marijuana and has Hank take him to a meth hotel to lecture him about marijuana as "the gateway drug"; and in episode 104 ("Cancer Man"), when the maid discovers a joint in the Pinkman house and the parents kick Jesse out, never realizing that their younger, "trophy" son was the one who brought in the joint.

Throughout the series, there is an attitude of wicked irony taken toward all of the empty narratives of the therapeutic culture that engulfs us: right from the opening moments of episode 101 ("Pilot"), when, reacting to Walt's yet-to-be-diagnosed lung-cancer cough, Skyler says, "Did you remember to take your echinacea?" The world has become overloaded with half truths, with clichés, with largely unattributable thoughts and emotions. In a scene in episode 106 ("Crazy Handful of

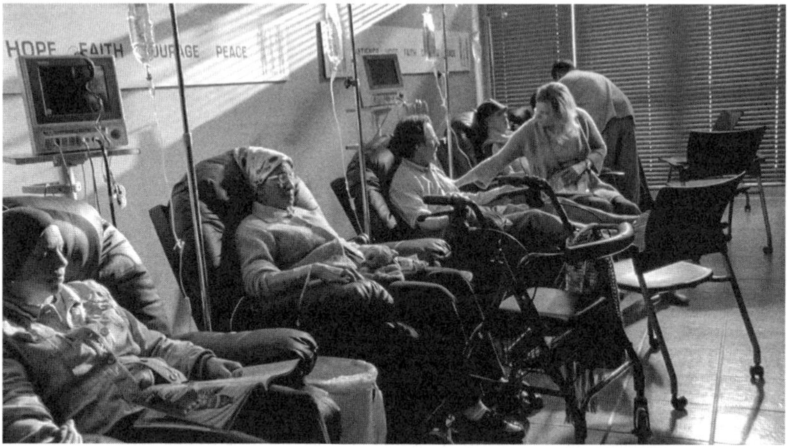

1.2. Group chemotherapy: "HOPE FAITH COURAGE PEACE"

Nothin'"), four people sit in recliners lined up along a wall; above each recliner dangles a bag of IV solution (fig. 1.2). On the wall behind the participants in this scene of mass chemotherapy hang rectangular placards bearing the words "HOPE FAITH COURAGE PEACE." But in this context, where are these words coming from? The words might just as well be hanging from the wall of a funeral parlor, which indeed is where a diagnosis of stage-four cancer is most likely to lead our thoughts.

An attention to narrative gaps and intensive passages can have the effect of clearing away these habitual ways of seeing the world. André Bazin, the great postwar theorist of cinematic realism, wrote of Italian neorealism that it was as if, our eyes having been covered with layers of grime from habitual perception, neorealist aesthetics swept away this distorting "film" and gave us a more immediate perception of the objects surrounding us.[32] But Bazin also praised classical Hollywood directors such as William Wyler and Orson Welles. In other words, even in the more narratively driven works of commercial cinema, certain aesthetic strategies are likely to shake us out of our habitual ways of seeing. And in fact, the contemporary television series is making ever more clear that the extended nature of its presentation, its engagement over longer periods of time with the spaces and objects of everyday life, might very well work in its favor in any project to "reprogram" our sensorium.[33]

While the question of what's going to happen next will no doubt always drive viewers' engagement with the shows, a television of mise-en-scène demonstrates, for example, how—amid the endless chattering of the people around us—a new thought or idea is born. (In episode 501 ["Live Free or Die"], as Walter and Mike stand at opposite ends of the frame arguing pointlessly about how to solve the problem of Gus Fring's laptop, which has been impounded by the police and is filled with incriminating evidence against them, the camera keeps an out-of-focus Jesse centered in the frame, sitting on a sofa behind and between them, and Jesse repeatedly tries to get them to hear his idea—"magnets!"—which remains inchoate until the rack focus pulls Jesse into clear view. Here is visualized the birth of a thought: the thought doesn't come from the drawn-out discussion in the foreground, but flashes up from the background, where we least expect it.) Or how, in an array of mundane objects of everyday life, one of those objects will leap out of its context and enter into a wholly new relationship with characters and actions. In short, how invisible forces become actualized.[34]

The breaches or gaps in narrative causality that are central to *Breaking Bad*'s aesthetic strategies are, in fact, announced rather obviously when Walt adopts the street name "Heisenberg." It doesn't take a quantum physicist to know that Walt is taking as his namesake the scientist who proposed that there is a fundamental and inherent uncertainty connected to the most basic building blocks of the universe, such that the closer we come to pinning down one variable, the more uncertain its complementary variable becomes.[35] In terms of art, we could say that while narrative presents us with a linear set of relations (a "chain," more aligned to Newtonian mechanics), the complementary forces of mise-en-scène introduce gaps and uncertainties deep within the heart of these story lines (more aligned to quantum physics).

One of the ways that *Breaking Bad* follows through on this disruption is via its unique approach to the cold openings, or teasers, which we learn to read as having a nonlinear (and unpredictable) relationship to the episode to follow.[36] While sometimes the teaser gives us a partial and condensed version of what will turn out to be the climax of the particular episode, at other times it is a direct continuation of the action that occurred at the end of the previous episode—for example, in episodes 202 ("Grilled") and 203 ("Bit by a Dead Bee"), where 202 ends with Walt and Jesse walking off into the desert after Tuco has been shot by Hank, and the 203 teaser continues this action as the two hitchhike to the supermarket, where Walter strips naked and feigns his "fugue state." Sometimes, as in several teasers during season two, the teaser presents us with fragments of the final, climactic moments of the season. At other times, the teaser gives us a flashback, either to an episode earlier in the series or to situations that occurred long before the story begins. Finally, the teaser can be less attached to the narrative line, as in episode 207 ("Negro y Azul"), where the teaser is a music video of a Mexican narcocorrida song in which Walt improbably appears at various points. (Yet another version of this style of teaser occurs in episode 309 ["Kafkaesque"], where we see what appears to be a television commercial for Los Pollos Hermanos in which the falling pieces of chicken dissolve into falling meth crystals, after which the teaser provides us with information about how the drugs are being shipped; and in episode 312 ["Half Measures"], where a montage of the meth whore Wendy turning tricks for her habit is set to the bouncy tune of the 1967 Association hit "Windy" and is ultimately given a narrative value when Jesse uses her routine to attempt to poison the drug dealers responsible for having had the minor Tomás kill Jesse's friend Combo.)

This nonlinearity at the macro level of the episode finds its counterpart at the micro level via the ways that mise-en-scène introduces gaps and undecidability in the cause-effect logic of narrative. Let's take as an example the climactic scene in episode 212 ("Phoenix"), when Walt hesitates as he witnesses Jane choke to death on her vomit while unconscious from a heroin high. What is surprising about reactions to this scene is how often and how readily viewers assume Walt made an explicit decision to look on as Jane died. Indeed, in an interview with Vince Gilligan, Bryan Cranston, and Aaron Paul, film critic David Edelstein asserted that this was the moment in which his spectatorial identification with Walter White was ruptured beyond repair. But what we learn in the interview is that Gilligan and Cranston revised the action of the scene in such a way as to build indeterminacy into Walt's reactions. As initially written, Walt *was* a deliberate agent in Jane's death: upon hearing her begin to choke while she was lying on her side, Walt was to place his hand on her shoulder and slowly push her onto her back, and so ensure that she would likely choke to death. But as finally played by Cranston, Jane's death was—in Cranston's words—"an accident," as Walter White becomes paralyzed by all the conflicting desires that are coursing through him in this charged moment.[37] Importantly for our argument, what this reveals is that the series chooses not to clarify the meanings of actions by writing in facile cues to provide logical explanation. In this way, the indeterminacy that is built into the aesthetic idea of the shooting is very much akin to the aesthetics of the art cinema growing out of Italian neorealism. Bazin made fun of Hollywood's "doorknob shot," the point of view of the convict to be executed at daybreak, which forces the spectator to reduce a complex situation to a simple thought.[38] By the mid-1950s, with Roberto Rossellini's collaborations with Ingrid Bergman, the art film was able to achieve the elimination of what I would call "doorknob shots of the mind," which provide the spectator with facile psychological motives with which to oversimplify the complexity of human action. In much of contemporary television—think, for example, of procedurals such as the *CSI* franchise—the doorknob shot is often achieved by a veritable feat of forced scriptwriting, in which two characters somehow manage to telegraph to the viewers all sorts of tidbits of narrative information while seeming to be having a casual conversation.

What do we see in Jane's death sequence in 212? About a dozen shots unfold from the moment in a high overhead shot when Jane begins coughing in her sleep to the episode blackout. However, roughly six shots before this overhead shot, when Walt is trying to awaken Jesse from his heroin slumber by shaking his arm, this action inadvertently causes the passed-out Jane to roll from her side onto her back. Had this chain of events not occurred, she would have been much less vulnerable to death by suffocation. When Walt notices what is happening with Jane, he rushes around the bed to Jane's side, his hands extended toward her body. We see a close-up of Walt's face and then a shot of him beside the bed, his hand paralyzed over Jane's body. Within seconds, it is over: Jane is dead. As Walt looks at Jane's body, he suddenly covers his mouth as a tear rolls down his left cheek (fig. 1.3).

Clearly, the moment that produces the gap or breach in the narrative

1.3. Walt's tear indexes an invisible affective change

occurs in the shots where we see Walt's hands paralyzed and unable to act. From our point of view, though, the aesthetic interest here is not in how easily we can explain the gap, but in the ways in which the gap holds open interpretive possibilities. For example, it is easy to imagine a person in such a situation who might hesitate simply because they would not know what to do, or who would be paralyzed for any number of reasons that wouldn't make them morally reprehensible. While we know that Walt had reasons to want Jane dead, we don't get any doorknob shots here. Instead, we get something much more aesthetically interesting: the tear that, like the bubbles in a pot of water about to boil, is the index of an intensive change. How are we to understand this tear?

At this mark of something invisible having happened within Walter White, a number of narrative strands within the episode coalesce, if only to spiral into a vortex of indetermination. Yes, Walter had ample reason for wanting Jane out of the way: she seemed to be not only leading Jesse astray but also taking Jesse away from him, and after learning of the money owed Jesse, she suddenly becomes the femme fatale, threatening to expose Walt's criminal activity. Yet this is also the episode in which Walt becomes a father to a baby girl—even if a drug deal forces him to miss the baby's birth. As if to allay his own guilt over this, after the baby is brought home, he picks her up one night and, cradling her in his arms, brings her to the bundles of cash he's made on the drug deal, as if to say, "See how Daddy is providing for you?" (not seeming to realize that the whole scenario is bordering on the psychotic). This patriarchal concern over the vulnerability of the female offspring is then taken up toward the end of the episode, when Walt has a random conversation with a man whom we know to be Jane's father about parents' charged relationships to their children, before they veer off into a discussion of possible life on Mars. In all these cases, ordinary human interchange seems to approach a limit beyond which the world might collapse (into psychosis, into film noir, into the unknown); the tear Walt sheds at Jane's deathbed is a condensation of all this.

Such is the uncertainty principle that the series introduces into simple narrative cause and effect. Thus in episode 213 ("ABQ"), we finally see how the pink teddy bear shown floating in the Whites' pool in several teasers throughout the season got there: it is the debris from a plane crash that occurs when Jane's grieving father—an air traffic controller—spaces out before his control screen at work. Something akin to a butterfly effect is at work: actions at a distance, where a slight gesture over here (like shaking a drugged-out Jesse) unintentionally "causes" two planes to collide over there. This logic perfectly mimics the structure of feeling of the subject of contemporary neoliberal (and networked) economies, whose every slight action seems potentially to have disastrous consequences in the long run, but who can never be certain how any one action can be significant enough to affect the outcome.[39] The teddy bear itself becomes the odd leftover in this sequence of events, falling as it does right into Walter's backyard. The circuit of affect that began with the tear welling from Walter's left eye now finds its counterpart in the child's toy seared from the flames of a horrible crash, its own left eye pulled out of its socket and ultimately sucked into the filtration vent of the swimming pool.

This concern with the leftover, the remainder, the surplus, is the logical counterpart to the focus on intensive changes in the mise-en-scène: the leap from one state to another always leaves behind the tear, the residue in the meth pipe, the smudge of Skyler's mudpack on the refrigerator after Walt's unwanted sexual advance in the kitchen. But it is precisely this logic that Walter White cannot accept or comprehend:

he dreams of a pure accountability, where nothing falls through the cracks of an absolute cause-effect chain. (In this sense, his embrace of the Heisenberg uncertainty principle connects only to the world outside the Law, to the renegades, the abjects, and the "others" who lie outside the radar screen of "White" America.) The logic of the surplus is directly articulated in a flashback that occurs within the teaser to episode 103, when Walt remembers being in a graduate school classroom lab, breaking down with a fellow grad student the chemical composition of the human body. No matter how many elements they go through, a fraction of a percent of the human body's composition remains unaccounted for. Walt cannot accept the suggestion of his classmate that perhaps the soul is what accounts for the missing percentage.

This flashback is triggered by a particularly gruesome task Walt and Jesse are engaged in: cleaning up the entrails of the murdered Emilio, now partially dissolved by hydrofluoric acid, after the acid has eaten through the tub and floor of the second-story bathroom where Jesse had attempted to dispose of the body (in 102). The "magical" properties of hydrofluoric acid are, to be sure, the stuff of many a schoolboy's morbid jokes; here, however, the use of the acid is clearly connected to the dream of a perfect exchange, the abolishment of that supplement or trace that renders all of human life fallen. We may be waiting for Walter White to break bad, but isn't this act—this utter disrespect of the dead, such that, far from even denying Emilio his right to be buried, Walter wants to efface any trace of his remains—the most fundamentally inhuman act of the series?

As if to underscore this point, the act is repeated in an even more horrific way in episode 506 ("Buyout"), when the gang disposes of the motorbike—and by extension, the body—of the boy Todd shoots and kills after the boy has witnessed the "great train robbery" of methylamine. This cold opening to 506 gives us a particularly strong instance of resonance, or transference of energies, in the mise-en-scène. The scene is presented with no dialogue, only eerie music in the background, as a dump truck filled with desert clay pulls into the frame. A few implements from the robbery are unearthed from the truck, and then the motorbike of the murdered boy is pulled out. The men begin dismembering the motorbike and placing parts in the large plastic barrel resis-

1.4. Exhuming the boy

tant to hydrofluoric acid. The images of dismemberment become more intense as, arriving at the last large pieces, they must resort to using a power saw on the tire and a welding torch on the frame to break down the bike. Then Todd moves to the mound of dirt in the truck, feeling around until the boy's hand is unearthed (fig. 1.4), and a second plastic container appears next to the first. Yes, the motorbike is a stand-in for the boy, but it oversimplifies the scene to turn the bike into such a metaphor, because this reduces the affective energies escalating through the scene to a strictly narrative purpose. Finally, the appearance of the boy's hand evokes an entire tradition of surrealist films (and even American horror: think of the final shot of Brian De Palma's *Carrie* [1976]) to create a strange reversal: the body, which properly should remain buried, is instead going to be dug up (offscreen) and dissolved.

But notwithstanding the hubris that has turned Walter White into a monster as early as episode 102, this dream of the abolishment of the leftover, of the perfect coincidence of words and meaning, signifier and signified, cause and effect, production and consumption, is one of the fundamental fantasies of human life. Today, however, with just-in-time production processes wedded to advertising that promises to be tailored to a single, unique human, it might seem that the realization of this fantasy is just around the corner.

2 The House

Mise-en-scène, as we have seen, is an operation of orchestration: on the one hand, we have all the variables of the apparatus (camera position, lens, light, movement), and on the other, all the objects and bodies distributed in the world (even if the world is a studio set). The entire system is a highly dynamic one: any change in one of the elements on either side of the equation alters the energies present in the entire frame. One of the innovations of *Breaking Bad* is the extensive deployment of handheld shots, especially challenging in a series largely shot on 35mm film, with its relatively heavy cameras.[1] (The handheld work is easily seen in the "dismemberment" teaser to episode 506 ["Buyout"], for example.) Freeing the camera from the encumbrances of tripods, cranes and dollies, or Steadicam facilitates the creation of intensive mise-en-scène, as it allows the camera to continually find the most expressive position for an action, whereas a locked-down camera tends to force the scene to unfold via a few preconceived setups. The handheld camerawork becomes particularly effective in shooting the long, dramatic confrontations between characters so as to show us the constantly shifting power relations as they unfold in a scene.

In film studies, one school of thought argues that the cinema—from its origins in the 1890s through to its heyday in the ages of the new waves—was the central technology for allowing us to negotiate the changes wrought by the rapid modernizations that occurred throughout the twentieth century. Given the accelerated speeds of life brought about by the train and the automobile; the heightened sensations created by the influx of people to urban centers; and the urban dweller's continual exposure to newness, whether in technological inventions or encounters with ethnic, racial, or sexual "others," the cinema's ability to orchestrate objects in the world allowed it to function as a kind of central nervous system of modernity. Walter Benjamin was one of the earliest thinkers to develop this view of cinema, which is evident in his famous statement: "Our bars and city streets, our offices and furnished rooms, our railroad stations and our factories seemed to close relentlessly around us. Then came film and exploded this prison-world with the dynamite of the split second, so that now we can set off calmly on journeys of adventure among its far-flung debris."[2] In other words, the cinema broke apart our habitual views of the world and then reassembled the pieces in such a way as to reprogram our sensorium, to show us how to live amid the new conditions of modernity. And while this procedure of disassembly–reassembly is often thought of in connection with editing or montage, it is critical for our purposes to understand how central mise-en-scène is to this entire process: editing is most expressive when it unfolds the energies held together within the frame.

The cinema, then, was instrumental in "programming" us to adapt and perhaps even thrive in the modernizing spaces of the twentieth century, whether it was through the single woman negotiating the freedoms and dangers of the streets of Manhattan in George Loane Tucker's *Traffic in Souls* (1913), or through the camera negotiating the tenements, street markets, and gangs of the immigrant neighborhoods of downtown New York in D. W. Griffith's *The Musketeers of Pig Alley* (1912). It is this property of cinema that gets reinvented over and over again, as the various new waves that sweep across the globe attempt to make sense of the shantytowns that sprang up around Rome in the 1950s (Pier Paolo Pasolini's *Mamma Roma* [1962]), the construction of the high-rises in the banlieues surrounding Paris (Jean-Luc Godard's *Alphaville* [1965] and *Two or Three Things I Know about Her* [1967]), or the real estate bubble that transformed the landscape of Taipei in the 1980s (Tsai Ming-liang's *Vive L'Amour* [1994]). Often, this sense-making process is thought of as "mapping": the cinema constructs maps that allow us to act and move about within our world.

The question for us then becomes, To what extent does a newly cinematic television—and specifically, *Breaking Bad*—accomplish a similar kind of mapping for the twenty-first century, and for a new stage of capitalism that is centered on financialization, the production of spectacle, and the management of affect? Variously called late capitalism, postindustrial capitalism, or postmodern capitalism, this economy is characterized by vast but largely invisible flows of information, of data, and even of affective states (via Facebook, Twitter, etc.). In fact, the flows of contemporary postnetwork television are linked up to all of these other flows, and as such it is difficult to imagine television functioning as the central nervous system of postmodernity the way we characterized cinema's relation to an earlier modernity; televisual flow is seamlessly integrated into both the macro-level flows of contemporary capitalism and the micro-level flows that set the rhythms for how we live everyday life. Thus, rather than the "dynamite of the split second," televisual flow gives us the steady humming of the present, helping to effect a synchronization between lived social time and the instantaneous global flows of information.

This is the idea underwriting the notion—advanced by philosopher Jacques Derrida and his student Bernard Stiegler—that television is engaged in the manufacture of the present. Derrida coined the neologism "artifactuality"—a combination of artifice and actuality (from the French, meaning "what is happening now")—to describe this process: the present, far from being raw sense data, comes to us already mediated.[3] We can thus say that televisual flow marks a decisive shift in the evolution of the moving-image apparatus: while the cinema at its best reconfigured the objects and spaces of a modernity that was "out there," television's vast penetration into the spaces of everyday life (as well as its potential for "liveness") makes it complicit in constructing the very "there" itself. It is a case where the map begins to coincide with, and create, the territory.

It seems that some sort of "interruptor" would be required to allow for respite from this vicious circle. If the cinematic—in all the specificities developed in chapter 1—is acting as this interruptor in *Breaking Bad*, what does this mean? As I have argued, *Breaking Bad*'s constant invocation of the film canon is not a case of blank citation or postmodern recycling, but rather a means for developing cinematic ideas. But the series is still situated within the parameters of television. Its long-form seriality means that we live with the series; it unfolds within the rhythms of our everyday lives. In this way, it might just allow us, over the course of several years, to slowly disengage from the manufactured present. Slowly, our own houses and the objects cluttering our lives begin to look different to us; our clothes begin to say something other than what we intended.

This is an aesthetic response at its most philosophically rich level: aesthetics not as a style or a look, but as an ongoing engagement with invention and indeterminate judgments. The rest of this chapter and the next will look at the houses and the objects of *Breaking Bad*, specifically in the ways in which they are central to constructing an aesthetic response to the world of the twenty-first century.

Has any other television series created such reverberant, affective domestic spaces? Production designer Mark Freeborn has talked about how the production team wanted to turn the White house into "a kind of tragic character" in its own right.[4] And it is certainly a disturbing moment when, in the teaser to episode 509 ("Blood Money"), we see the house that we have "lived in" for five years in utter ruination: boarded up, filled with graffiti, gutted by urban scavengers. This teaser can be seen as a bookend to the teaser of 313 ("Full Measure"), where the house is shown by a realtor to the newly married Walt and Skyler: here the house is empty, but "pregnant" with possibility, so that what disturbs us is knowing how all this possibility will have been actualized in the comfortable ugliness of their furnishings. This "tragic" evolution we see in the White house is narratively driven, but as such it is only an instance (at the macro level) of the way the series renders all its domestic spaces as (at the micro level) spaces of becoming, accomplished through the very cinematic means of lighting and camera that I have outlined so far.

We can think of the various domestic spaces of *Breaking Bad* along an axis of inertia–speed, but with the caveat that the mise-en-scène is always capable of accelerating or decelerating the affective dimensions of the space. The White house would have a high degree of inertia: we quickly become accustomed to the comfortable slowness produced by the well-worn furniture, the afghan that's always draped over the sofa, the ugly, earth-toned plaids of the drapery, the useless but decorative folding screen, the early-American "dinette set" that was probably picked up at a yard sale or held over from graduate school days. We know from the earliest episodes that Skyler is a creative writer manquée. We doubt she has ever published; she certainly is never seen writing, or worrying about making the time to write. We may surmise that she was an English major who now takes the occasional fiction-writing class in order to give her that je ne sais quoi that will keep her feeling somehow still "in the game." The furnishings in the house reflect this: it is as if one can be ostentatious about one's makeshift surroundings as long as one tells oneself that it reflects a life devoted to higher, more ethereal concerns. The White house thus gives us a secure home base from which we can roam; but at the same time, the inertia of the house works to heighten our anxiety once the interior, familial order falls increasingly under the threat of invasive violence as Walter pursues—with much more success than does Skyler—his own "artistic vocation."

Hank and Marie's house—no doubt due to the utter impossibility of their having an original thought, to the sheer doggedness with which they indulge their obsessive-compulsive disorders—is aspirational, but it doesn't quite make it to the level of contemporary chic. Still, the space is open and so produces more of a sense of speed and mobility than the cluttered White house—ironic, after Hank's lower body becomes paralyzed from an encounter with the Salamanca brothers. Jesse, in keeping with his age and personality, cycles through a series of living arrangements, but after his parents throw him out of his dead aunt's house, his living quarters always seem makeshift and transitory, dominated by the large electronic screens and speakers that introduce speed and flow into the space.

Stewart Lyons, unit production manager for the series, has said that the White house is bigger on the inside than it is on the outside.[5] On the one hand, this is in keeping with a lot of Sunbelt home architecture: even in an older city like Atlanta, one often sees a house that from the outside appears to be not much more than a cottage, but inside has a surprising number of spacious rooms. On the other hand, it is an effect endemic to the cinema itself: the inside—here a studio set with moveable walls—must be large enough to allow the extraction of the maximum expressivity of the space, given the cameras and lenses being used. It's a requirement for mise-en-scène once the camera and lighting are liberated from the fixed positions in the traditional television studio.

Lyons has also said that in the White house, there are "doors leading nowhere."[6] Again, one would expect this in a studio set, where fixtures, appliances, and so on, need only be functional when they must be used within the scene. But the fact that the set design can be made to "cheat" for the camera can lead to unforeseen logical complication for viewers and especially fans, as exemplified in a wiki discussion thread concerning how many bathrooms the White house has.[7] The only bathroom that we see is what would be called a master bath adjoining the main bedroom: we know one enters it through a louvered door inside the parents' bedroom. (The layout is clearly seen in episodes 508 ["Gliding over All"] and 509 ["Blood Money"], when Hank discovers the *Leaves of Grass* volume resting on the toilet tank; and it is used to great dramatic effect when in 302 ["Caballo Sin Nombre"] the axe-bearing Salamanca brothers invade the house while Walter is in the shower, and the two brothers, intent on murdering Walt, sit calmly on the bed waiting for him to emerge.) Clearly, though, there must be another bathroom: it would be inconceivable that Walt Jr. would have to traipse through his parents' bedroom every time he needed to use the bathroom. Along the sides of the corridor that ends in the doorway to the master bedroom, there are three doors: two along the right wall and one along the left. From this we might surmise that the two right-side doors are the doors to the children's rooms, while the door on the left opens onto a second bath. But the few times we enter that space, we find that it is a small utility room (with the defective water heater that ultimately gets replaced, and a trapdoor leading to the crawl space below the house). The necessary second bathroom is unlocatable. Here is a case where the left-side door, the door that "leads nowhere," can take on multiple functions, as long as it is mostly closed: behind that door we can presume to be anything that is missing visually but required logically.

This, then, is an overview of the most regularly seen domestic spaces in the series: in a sense, the raw material for the elaboration of a mise-en-scène that will introduce change and becoming into the houses.

2.1. The White house: The light cannot fully illuminate the space

Given that the series tends to favor the long shot over the close-up in developing a sequence, we get plenty of views of the various living spaces from all angles, and often this means that the lighting of the space is prioritized over the lighting of an actor. In the case of the White house, full light is rare except in the event of parties or family gatherings. While the house seems open to natural light from all sides (as well as from three skylights in the hallway), even during the day the house is rarely bright, but rather is penetrated by shafts of light that leave much of the space relatively obscure (fig. 2.1). It is as if the light cannot fully illuminate the world; this is the series' debt to expressionism. Sometimes the surface of the pool, or the fabric of the curtains, is used to create vibratory or pulsating light on the walls (as, for example, in the opening shot of 509, when the camera slowly moves toward the closed door of the bathroom we know Hank is in, and the walls of the bedroom glimmer with the play of natural light coming through the window curtains; or the night shot in 508, when Skyler approaches Walt sitting alone by the pool, and the walls pulsate with reflected blue light).

These two lighting ideas—which can be traced back to the postwar melodrama and film noir of classical Hollywood—suggest that the White house is beleaguered from both within and without. This is in contrast to Hank and Marie's house, whose open design emphasizes surfaces and full, even light. The light here provides a "false" clarity, however, insofar as Hank and Marie are unable to see complexity or irony: the sources of Marie's kleptomania are buried and locked away for good, while Hank, in a conversation over contraband Cuban cigars seized by the DEA and now being enjoyed by Hank and Walt, cannot comprehend the fundamental arbitrariness of the law (107, "A No-Rough-Stuff-Type Deal").

Jesse presents us with much more variability in his living spaces, which range from the staidly decorated house of the now-dead aunt (season one) who gave him living rights to the place because of his ongoing loyalty to her, up (or rather down) to complete homelessness early in season two. Jesse is the only major character who can see "from the inside" the alternate worlds of drug users, worlds that exist side by side with the "normal" world: the seedily furnished rooms of the 1950s-moderne meth motel; the abandoned buildings taken over and become shooting galleries; the church-basement-style rehab centers and twelve-step programs that peddle both victimization and authenticity. That Jesse more and more assumes the moral center of the universe of *Breaking Bad* is thus quite telling: perhaps it's because of his very involvement with drugs that he is able to see through the platitudes of official culture and the viciousness of the gangs. He's certainly the only main character who can actually see a homeless person.

Jesse's stint of homelessness occurs in season two, when his parents, in an act of venality disguised as tough love, sell the house he believes his aunt bequeathed (at least informally) to him. Jesse claims—and we have no reason to doubt his story, and every reason to doubt his mother's—that he took on the responsibility of caring for his sick aunt after his mother abandoned her. This accusation leads to a melodramatic encounter in which his mother slaps him and Jesse responds by calling her a bitch (204, "Down"). The edginess and innovation with which *Breaking Bad* handles the family melodrama can be seen as early as episode 104 ("Cancer Man"), when Jesse, after an attack of meth-induced paranoia, seeks refuge in his parents' house. When the cleaning woman discovers a joint in the house and reports it to the parents, Jesse ends up taking the blame even though—we discover later—the joint actually belonged to his younger brother, the model son. This one event illustrates perfectly how the series is able, in such an off-handed way, to orchestrate a complex web of power relations so that we see the entire "drug problem" in a more critical light.

To begin with, we have the Latina maid who must, by virtue of circumstance, treat the discovery of the joint as fraught with danger. Whether she is undocumented or simply at the lowest rung of the economic ladder, she knows that the presence of even one joint could easily have life-shattering consequences for her—as it does later (in 106 ["Crazy Handful of Nothin'"] for the Native American janitor at the high school. Indeed, the expression on her face when she alerts the parents to her discovery (in a brilliantly acted turn) shows us just what a double bind she is in: What if the parents, for whatever reason, turn on her? Just as with the parents at the high school meeting about the chem lab thefts (107), Jesse's parents can only interpret the joint from within the frame of their own fantasy of what constitutes the "ideal family," which allows them to cast Jesse as the black sheep and pin all of their hopes on his younger brother. Whether they're in for a rude awakening with "Junior" we will never know. But what this little melodrama does reveal is that middle-class fantasies of the good life (which I think it is safe in this context to call entitlement, or "white privilege") are always likely to trump any engagement with reality, whether it be the reality of racism, class exploitation, or the generalized banality—especially accessible to smart teenagers—of American high school culture.

I will return to melodrama in due course. But first, while I've established some of the basic ways in which the various domestic spaces are visualized, I want to look at the specific ways in which the intensities or forces within the domestic spaces are achieved. We might begin by looking once again at thresholds: in the house these are materialized as doors, windows, hallways, and so on. In episode 201 ("Seven Thirty-Seven"), after Tuco's outburst of murderous violence against one of his henchmen, Walter begins to fear that Tuco's men are following him. The buildup begins one night when Walter, driving home from a meetup with a panicked Jesse (who has just purchased a handgun he has no idea how to use), steps from his parked car to pick up the newspaper in the driveway and hears the ignition of a vehicle starting. He looks down the street to see a black SUV, headlights off, idling a few doors down. When he takes a few steps in the direction of the SUV, the vehicle reacts by slowly moving backward, away from him, until it backs into a driveway to make a U-turn and drive away. Already, we are seeing how the pattern of action-reaction works to modulate the force fields in the image, forcing us into thought: the SUV retreats in the face of Walter's advance, and yet this movement just underscores Walter's powerlessness in the situation.

As the paranoia increases in the episode, the telephone becomes the first vehicle from which "the outside" invades domestic space: a venerable trope from film noir whose perhaps most frightening instance occurs in the kitchen of Fritz Lang's *The Big Heat* (1953), where the wife's answering the threatening call suggests that the entire family is in jeopardy. In episode 201, the first instance of this is a banal call from Marie that causes Walter to jump in panic after he's spent the night on guard at the front window. The next instance is more ominous: Hank, from the auto graveyard, sends Walt a picture of the dead bodies of Tuco's henchmen. Now Jesse gives his handgun to Walter, who rushes home thinking his family is in danger, only to find Skyler luxuriating in the bathtub. As he sits on the side of the tub and an annoyed and confused Skyler tries to find out what's going on with him, the conversation is interrupted by two short rings of his cell phone. Then, just as he is beginning to concoct some story for Skyler, the wall behind him lights up with reflected light. He looks through the open door to the bedroom and sees what must be car headlights coming through the window and moving across the wall (fig. 2.2). The "home invasion" is complete, and now Walt will join Jesse as a hostage of Tuco.

The climactic moments of season three (313, "Full Measure") present us with an even more elaborate orchestration of intensive thresholds and actions-at-a-distance. After having killed two of Gus's street dealers, both Walt and Jesse feel that Gus is going to move fast with his plan to get rid of them both. Jesse goes into hiding, while Gus insists that his protégé Gale return as Walt's assistant; once Gale learns Walt's cooking secrets, Walt can be disposed of. Walt's plan is thus to get rid of Gale as a way to at least temporarily prolong his own life, but just as he is leaving on the mission to kill Gale, he's sidelined by the lab guard Victor, who forces him to go to the lab, where Mike is waiting. Walt's time is up; Gus has decided to move forward.

2.2. Car lights from outside invade the house

As Mike and Victor stand in the lab with guns pointed at Walter, Walter tells them he'll give them Jesse. But this is a ruse, for when he gets Jesse on the phone, he informs Jesse of the emergency and tells him he must kill Gale immediately. Now comes a series of intensive relays in the mise-en-scène: Gale's cell phone begins to vibrate on his counter, but the water in the teakettle has just reached its boiling point and the kettle begins to whistle, drowning out the sound of the cell phone. Shortly thereafter, there is a knock on the door: Jesse is on the other side of the threshold. Jesse pulls a gun out of his waistband and points it at Gale as he crosses the threshold and moves into the apartment. Suddenly, the scene cuts to a long shot in which the still steaming teakettle is in the foreground, while the figures of Jesse and Gale are out of focus in the distant background (fig. 2.3). Why this seemingly unmotivated cut away from the dramatic center of the scene (especially since the rest of the scene will play out as crosscutting between medium shots of the two men)? Whatever the symbolism of the teakettle may be, it functions here as an intensive relay that allows energies to be redistributed across the images. Just as we've seen in chapter 1 in relation to the general deployment of mise-en-scène, now, in the domestic space of the home or apartment, we are continually being taken across thresholds: physical, emotional, mental, moral.

2.3. Intensive relay: Jesse crosses a threshold just as does the water in the kettle

This idea in fact becomes explicitly thematized in the teaser to 311 ("Abiquiu"), a flashback in which Jane takes Jesse to an exhibition of Georgia O'Keeffe paintings. Jesse chides Jane that O'Keeffe just kept painting the same door, over and over; for Jane, though, the door is never the same from one instance to the next, so that O'Keeffe approaches the door as an always new encounter. Jesse is looking at art in a "molar" way, as a simple representation, whereas Jane is arguably looking at the forces O'Keeffe was trying to capture. We can see how this disagreement in aesthetic response echoes back to Jacques Rancière's discussion of image and narrative presented in chapter 1, where narrative encourages us to subtract values from the image and thus to instrumentalize our perceptual apparatus: "a door is a door."

Perhaps the most complex orchestration of frames as thresholds—and one most clearly connected to the family melodrama—occurs at the climax of episode 411 ("Crawl Space"), when Walt appears to have a near psychotic break while lying in the crawl space under the house. The narrative background is this: A kind of rivalry of fathers develops over Jesse when Gus begins to take him under his wing, to the extent that he ends up making Jesse a key player in his successful plan to wipe out the remainder of the Mexican cartel. Meanwhile, Hank has discovered the connection between Los Pollos Hermanos and the local meth trade and is close to uncovering the dry-cleaning plant as a front for the lab. Walt feels increasingly expendable, as his brother-in-law is closing in on the lab while Jesse is now cooking meth for Gus on his own. Finally, when Gus has Walt tazed and brought to the desert, where he tells him his entire family will be wiped out if he interferes with Gus's plan to "deal with" Hank and the DEA, Walt decides to take the ultimate step and have himself and his family "disappeared." This is what leads him to the crawl space, where he tries to assemble the more than half-million dollars in cash he will need to make the transaction. Frantically grabbing money in the crawl space, he finds that there isn't enough, while upstairs a worried Skyler asks him what is happening.

Now the conversation proceeds by crosscutting, with Walter boxed in by the trapdoor, and with the low-angle shot of Skyler squeezing her between the frame of the trapdoor below and the frame of the doorway over her head. Walt's desperate screams soon turn into hysterical laughter, mostly shot from above, with the trapdoor creating a frame around him. At this point, the soundtrack takes up the increasing levels of intensity, first with a nondiegetic rhythmic beating, and then with the sound of the phone ringing. Skyler, disturbed and helpless, backs away from the trapdoor, in a low-angle shot in which her head is increasingly squeezed between the frame of the trapdoor below and the header of the door behind her, until she finally disappears from view (fig. 2.4). The scene now cuts to the hallway outside, as Skyler backs out of the closet while Marie, talking to the answering machine, reveals that the cartel is once again coming after Hank. What is clear so far—and the scene is not yet over—is that we are being moved through a series of passages, of heightening affective states, which the domestic architecture is now amplifying by creating a kind of echo chamber that—unlike the teakettle—allows nothing to escape. Indeed, Marie is crying, "When is this going to end?" just as Skyler traverses the corridor and picks up the phone.

While Skyler now tries to bring down the affective intensity, the scene leaves her to cut to an overhead shot through the trapdoor of a psychotically gripped Walt, his laughter subsiding into an ominous silence, as the camera cranes directly up toward the ceiling until the bare bulb of a hanging light fixture comes into frame (fig. 2.5).[8] Here, the mise-en-scène is extracting ever higher levels of intensity from the situation by

2.4 and 2.5. Mise-en-scène: No exit

way of a careful orchestration of the domestic space so that every movement is more and more boxed in, as if there is literally no exit. The very subtle effect of the hanging light bulb dropping into frame is to suggest a limit on the camera's upward movement, reminding us that there is a ceiling above.

These particular modulations of domestic space—the increasing claustrophobia, the imprisoning architectural features, the charged corridor, the sonic crescendo—are aesthetic features of the contemporary horror film; indeed, *Breaking Bad*'s production designers Robb Wilson King and Mark Freeborn have worked in the horror genre, in the films *Hostel 2* and *Final Destination 3*, respectively. Given the series' aesthetic appropriations, we could expect to see many such instances of genre crossing, among horror, crime, noir, and—most talked about by both creators and viewers—the western. If I am prioritizing melodrama here, it's not only because of my initial starting point, which is also the starting point of the entire series, at *Bigger Than Life*. It's because the aesthetics of melodrama—seen not as a genre but as a fundamental mode of experiencing modernity—comes to inflect all the popular genres. We have thus returned to the initial proposition of this chapter: that the cinema's vocation was to allow for a reconfiguration of bodies, objects, and spaces in such a way as to make sense of a changing world (via mise-en-scène). Melodrama extends and complicates this idea: first, because "music" in cinematic melodrama refers less to the nondiegetic swelling of instrumental music on the soundtrack than to the application of musical values—rhythm, tonality, color, and so forth—to the configuration of the scene; and second, because, via this procedure of mise-en-scène, the melodrama (to use Peter Brooks's apt phrase) "applies pressure to the gestures" of the human characters in order to uncover a hidden truth within the situation, unavailable to the characters because of their limited vision.[9]

Interestingly, Hollywood cinematic melodrama reached its height at the same historical moment (the 1950s) as the installation of television in the American home. As a number of scholars have noted, American commercial television quickly adopted formal strategies of segmentation that themselves might be considered melodramatic: most notably, a structure of shortened scenes punctuated by commercial breaks, which tends to encourage such melodramatic plot devices as sudden revelations and reversals, cliff-hangers, coincidences, and missed encounters. This strategy is directly related to television's need to deliver audiences to sponsors: it needed to find a way to command the attention of the "distracted spectator" located within a domestic sphere in which all kinds of other events are vying for the viewer's attention.[10]

Recently, some scholars have adopted the television writer's term "beat" to describe and analyze how this segmentation of narrative works in more contemporary television. As Michael Newman defines the term—a description taken up by Linda Williams in her argument about melodrama in *The Wire*—the beat seems to be synonymous with the "scene," as long as we see the latter as a unified spatial-temporal block. (In this sense, television's definition of the beat differs considerably from the definition used in the theater, as I will discuss later.) Newman notes that a typical episode of a dramatic series contains between twenty and forty beats, and that a typical beat lasts about two minutes. Narrative strands must be parceled out across many beats through the episode, which induces the writers to introduce complications, twists, and reversals in the narrative.[11] Williams directly takes up these ideas in her book on *The Wire*, first noting how this parceling out of the narrative follows the logic of melodrama, and then showing how—despite the claim that "it's not TV, it's HBO"—a typical episode of *The Wire* has an average beat length surprisingly close to a typical episode of *Homicide*: in the cases she breaks down, the episode of *The Wire* actually has a shorter average beat length (at 1.02 seconds) than that of *Homicide* (at 1.6 seconds). The uniqueness of *The Wire*, she concludes, lies not so much in a disruption of the televisual rhythm we are accustomed to as in the expansion of the worlds that are allowed visibility in this series, worlds which are generally repressed from the narratives of more conventional television representation.[12]

We know that *Breaking Bad* disrupts this narrative system in a fundamental way, by regularly extending, sometimes greatly, the duration of the scene.[13] But in order to understand just what is at stake here from the point of view of mise-en-scène, it is useful to bring in the different conception of the beat that comes from the theater and is commonly used by actors and directors in breaking down and rehearsing a play. For the actor, beats occur many times during a scene: they mark points in the play where something happens that forces the actor to modify her or his objectives in light of a new totalized situation. In theoretical terms, the beat marks a shift in the affective relations on the stage, how the power to act is redistributed among the characters. There is clearly a subjective element in the way a particular actor breaks down the beats within a scene, which is why the director will have a beat breakdown that is more global, tracking broader changes in the overall distribution of power on the stage. But it is clear that on the stage, the beat measures an intensive shift in the overall situation.

In effect, then, the beat in theater divides up the scene into any number of thresholds, and here we can begin to see how this might translate to the moving image. In the cinematic mode of production, the actor's performance is more often than not broken up into pieces (which may or may not correspond to the actor's sense of the beats of the scene) and usually shot out of order. The role of unfolding the beats within a scene now devolves to the "camera-eye," and thus to the function of mise-en-scène as I have elaborated it in this book. Of course, there are times when a scene is shot in one long take (or a few long takes put together), and in this case, the actors' breakdowns of the beats will be crucial to guiding their performances. But in terms of the camera, two things can happen, often simultaneously: the camera can work with the actors' beats, emphasizing, underlining, heightening them by way of framing, movement, and so on; or the camera can widen the scope of the affective energies of the actors by engaging with the objects in the space (the teakettle) or the space as a whole (the crawl space). The very long scenes that are a regular feature of *Breaking Bad* are usually broken down into a number of shots, but the frequent use of the handheld camera allows the camera crew to insert itself among the bodies of the actors. By carefully observing the action in rehearsal, the camera crew can find the perfect positions from which to extract the intensities as they play out, or—to return to the words of Peter Brooks—to put pressure on the gesture in order to coax out its hidden meaning.

From this, we can begin to see specifically how film melodrama, especially the great cycle of family melodramas of postwar Hollywood, differs from its (early) television counterpart. Television, with its primary imperative to elicit attention from a distracted spectator within a domestic space itself demanding attention—and, we must add, with only the resources of a relatively small cathode ray tube and a low-fidelity speaker—evolves a system of segmentation of the action that inherently lends itself to a melodramatic sensibility. The televisual beats elicit and hold attention via continual shifts in space-time, sudden revelations, reversals, complications, and cliff-hangers, but these melodramatic traits occur at the level of the narrative that is unfolding. In the film melodramas of the 1950s, in contrast, and as Thomas Elsaesser has shown so brilliantly, the musicality of the melodramatic imagination is transferred to the visual elements of the mise-en-scène.[14]

Two things result from this. First, musical organization connects us to a sense of time as duration: we understand a musical phrase to be completed not by the counting out of musical beats per measure, but by the melodic progression of the phrase in relation to the key signature of the piece. (Jazz, for example, often plays with disjunctions between the expectations produced by the tempo and the resolution of the musical phrases: syncopation would be the simplest example of this.) Whereas the televisual beat tends toward the chronometric unfolding of time, in the experience of duration each moment is connected to the next until the phrase is completed.[15] Thus, for example, in Douglas Sirk's *Written on the Wind* (1956), when Marylee (Dorothy Malone) begins her ecstatic dance in her bedroom while her defeated father slowly climbs the stairs, collapses from a heart attack as he nears the top, and then tumbles down the staircase while Marylee continues her wild kicking as she then collapses onto a chair, the entire sequence forms a block of duration, creating a series of rising and falling movements that reach a crescendo and finally resolve.

The second result of durational time is that we get actions-at-a-distance, outside of the narrative's cause-effect chain. Once again music can provide an initial example, as when a melodic theme long resolved suddenly returns, but in a new variation and harmonic context. In *Rebel without a Cause* (Nicholas Ray, 1955), for example, the unstable or skewed vantage point that begins the film as Jim Stark (James Dean) lies drunk on the curb continually returns with variations: the mother upside-down on the balcony, the skewed staircase where the argument takes place, all the way to the planetarium that decenters all of human life.

Once again we are confronted with Rancière's distinction between narrative and non-narrative dimensions of the image. One can see how, up until recent technological and industrial shifts in television, the apparatus necessarily had to emphasize the narrative dimensions of the image and then parcel the images out in such a way as to maximize attention. And—although I recognize the dangers of constructing a monolithic theory of the apparatus—this aesthetic mode does integrate nicely into those larger theories that argue that television is involved fundamentally with the synchronization of social time and the production of the present. This aesthetic mode of handling the image persists in contemporary television, as Linda Williams has shown in her study of the beat structure of *The Wire*. But I am not arguing that the televisual apparatus is the “bad object” that relentlessly normalizes the viewer via its “zero-degree style,”[16] and that only a return to the cinematic can liberate us from this. For one thing, we are beginning to see studies of televisual aesthetics that discover ways in which, from within the standard aesthetic practices of television, durations can be produced, durations that open up to the viewer more expansive ways of inhabiting the lived time of the images.[17]

Amy Villarejo, in her book *Ethereal Queer*, directly takes on this problem of duration. On the one hand, she wants to take seriously the theoretical claims about the apparatus made by Stiegler and others, claims that run against the tenor of a television studies grounded in cultural studies; but on the other hand, she wants to understand the ways television inhabits us without turning us into zombies, via the openings that continually present themselves in relation to lived experience that is now irremediably entwined with images from the “ether.” As Villarejo puts it, “Synchronization is never total.”[18] She uses the figure of the queer to mark those moments when alternative temporalities, alternative histories, can emerge. This, for Villarejo, is the “interruptor” I put forward earlier, the interruptor that introduces a gap between the map and the territory and that is effected in *Breaking Bad* by the cinematic. Thus the cinematic is not the high coming to the rescue of the low, but rather quite simply this interruptor.

The question that remains is, How do the concerns that we associate with the melodramatic mode become actualized through the work of mise-en-scène in *Breaking Bad*? Villarejo ends her book with a veritable celebration of melodrama as “the domain of gesture, silence, longing, muted expression, and the inchoate” and goes on to say, “As a powerful processor of a shared sensorium, melodrama, like television, is productive: it is a mode of transformation that strains to express the inexpressible.”[19] Much of this connects to what I’ve argued is the central interest of *Breaking Bad*: the minute attention to affective states, and the reprogramming of the sensorium. But what is being produced or transformed? This is an especially urgent question when we consider how melodrama so often thwarts us in our phantasmatic pursuit of fullness: if only we could read those muted gestures, we might yet be happy, but alas, everything will come too late.

Here I believe an important intervention in the theory of melodrama, by Agustín Zarzosa, will be useful in our attempt to connect mise-en-scène to affect, and specifically in relationship to how melodrama productively works on the spectator. Taking his cues from Rancière and Gilles Deleuze, Zarzosa insists that we think of affect in the rigorous philosophical sense developed by Spinoza, in the *Ethics*.[20] Affect refers to forces or potentialities distributed throughout the spaces of the world: in the case of cinema, we've seen how mise-en-scène works to choreograph these forces. But how do the characters within the film connect to these forces? Faced with a given (affective) world, does a character feel an increased expressive power (in which case we say the person is happy), or does she feel diminished in expressive power (in which case the person is sad)? This increased or decreased power is not necessarily connected to how the character is acting: confronted with a certain affective reality, a character might very well "act out" in aggressive or otherwise inappropriate ways, precisely as a reaction to the sad affection coming out of a feeling of impotence, or from a demonic compulsion to repeat. Certainly, Tuco in the auto graveyard has great power to act, but he is a sociopath, and as such his actions are more akin to reflexes than they are to expressivity. The value assigned to an expression is directly in relation to its creativity; to actively pursue destruction should be seen as the result of a "bad interpretation" of the affective field surrounding the destructive person.

It is perhaps becoming clear how the above might make an intervention in moving-image melodrama (one particularly useful for a series like *Breaking Bad*, which constantly shifts the affective levels in its mise-en-scène). But before moving forward, a philosophical excursus seems necessary. We begin with the idea that every situation is embedded within an affective field (a mise-en-scène of forces) that demands from the characters an action. But the extent to which the action is free, or liberating, has to do with the ideas, or thoughts, we bring to bear on the situation. In Spinoza, ideas are adequate or inadequate to a situation, and it's the action that comes from an inadequate idea that thwarts our achievement of happiness. "The family," for example, is an inadequate idea in *Breaking Bad* (just as it is in so many of the melodramas of post-war classical Hollywood).

Elsaesser's canonical essay on American film melodramas of the 1950s clearly shows us how the characters' ideas are the very things blocking them from understanding the real causes of their situations, and thus also preventing them from acting in such a way as to set themselves free. Elsaesser writes that "the poverty of the intellectual resources in some of the characters is starkly contrasted with a corresponding abundance of emotional resources, and . . . one sees them helplessly struggling inside their emotional prisons with no hope of realizing to what degree they are victims of their society." In a particularly resonant characterization of the films of Vincente Minnelli, he notes how a character will attempt to construct a world in the image of an inner self, only to find that world to be uninhabitable![21] This is one way to understand Walter White: his inner world insists that every infinitesimal be accounted for, which then forces him into a constant agonistic relationship to the outer world when it doesn't comply. "Heisenberg" as a signifier might have led him to an adequate idea, but in keeping with melodrama, he is unable to comprehend his own instinctual understanding of the world and turn it into an adequate idea.

One might at this point argue that this view of melodrama is better discussed as ideology: Aren't all these inadequate ideas simply the expression of the dominant ideology, and therefore wouldn't ideological critique be a more suitable avenue to pursue in relation to melodrama? In fact, Elsaesser's essay is decidedly oriented toward understanding melodrama in such ideological terms, in keeping with where film theory was in the early 1970s. And I would hardly argue with the fact that these inadequate ideas are ideological to the core. Of course the family represents ideology at its most fundamental level: it is the unit of social reproduction in the capitalist economy and as such becomes a central figure in all forms of popular culture, especially television. However, to say that "the family" is an inadequate idea provides us with an invitation to explore—in a direct, immanent way—exactly what its inadequacies are, and to experimentally test what ideas might be adequate to our reality. Ideology critique now becomes practical, deeply bound up with our immanent experience of everyday social relations. Moving-image melodrama is especially suited to this because, through mise-en-scène, it sets up a conflict between the affective rhythms of the scenes and how those are interpreted or assigned value. This, I would conclude, is what Villarejo means when she celebrates the transformative potential of melodrama.

So, for example, we say that in *Breaking Bad*, "the family" is an inadequate idea. It isn't just the way in which Walter White's repeated invocations of the family are so hollow, so disconnected from what he is actually doing—although one might conclude that he got this notion of family from a too-literal understanding of Francis Ford Coppola's *Godfather* films.[22] But in *Breaking Bad* familial relations begin to extend outward to encompass the entirety of the world. Walt and Jesse pass through every variation of the father-son relationship. But from the beginning, Hank stands in as a second, "virile" father for Walt Jr. (and interestingly ends up mirroring Junior when he loses the ability to "stand on his own two feet"); together, the childless Hank and Marie end up taking in the kids, ostensibly for the children's safety but always tinged with their own unmet needs. Against all this stands the Salamanca family, the one that most clearly actualizes that in *The Godfather*—the family as criminal enterprise, one in which the woman is rigorously excluded. (Aside from the prostitutes at the party massacre in episode 410 ["Salud"], do we ever see a woman in the Salamanca clan?)

Then there is the great homosexual series: Gus with his "partner" in a horrific flashback to a time before the series commences; Gus as "mentor" to Gale; even, it could be argued, the neo-Nazi gang Walt ends up aligned with. Todd—perhaps realizing how limited a set of choices his own family offers him—doggedly tries to get Walt to take him under his wing, while earlier in the series, Gale achingly yearns to be validated by Walt. Could it be that Walter senses in Gale's desire a perverse excess, one that has the potential to expose "white normality" as a sham? This would be in keeping with Jacques Lacan's formulation of perversion as "père-version," "the version of the father." For Gale is the one who gives Walt the gift that ultimately will undo his entire universe: a volume of *Leaves of Grass*, poetry that not only "sings the body electric" but more specifically celebrates sexual expression among men and even asserts the pedagogical dimensions of such relations.

Walter White is "the other W.W."—as Hank, in a bit of aggressive play, suggests. But what possesses Walt to install the incriminating volume in, of all places, the bathroom, where it sits above the toilet as a curated bathroom read? Walter White, of course, is an anal character par excellence: his obstinacy, obsession with contaminants (310, "Fly"), punctiliousness, and fixation on money all attest to this. Long before Walt begins his meth career, Jesse is onto this aspect of Walt's character: when he goes back to his parents' house in episode 104 ("Cancer Man"), he looks through his old high school papers and comes across a cartoon of his then teacher that he drew on the back of a failing chemistry exam, in which Walt, pants at his ankles, is being penetrated by some sort of laboratory measuring cylinder. So when Walt is confronted by the ideas of that other Walt, with the thought that the relations between men might be organized in some other way, he finds the ideas insistent enough that he cannot simply get rid of the volume (which will connect him to Gale's notebook, filled with incriminating evidence of his drug career), but he doesn't have enough self-clarity to understand why he has put the volume on the toilet (it is so naturally "in its place" for Walt that he doesn't notice it there in a scene in episode 508).

Because of these variations in familial relations, the "family," as Walt keeps using the word, is an inadequate idea. But we also see how this idea has acquired such a general currency that it comes to insinuate itself into all these different modes of relationality. It is as if the notion of the family is at once trying to move beyond the limitations of its (contemporary American) "nuclear" formation and continually occluding the possibilities for some other idea to emerge.

To return to Zarzosa's theorization of melodrama, we can say that at the first, most primary level, we have the world of affects, the virtual potentialities that inhabit the spaces between bodies in the world. These affects make demands on the characters; they invite the characters to action. But at the same time, the characters carry with them all sorts of preexisting ideas that impose themselves on the situation. Whether an action is fully expressive ("active" in the best sense), or whether it is blocked or misdirected ("reactive" in the Nietzschean sense), has to do with the extent to which characters can see beyond the "inverted optics" of their inadequate ideas and creatively engage with the situation at hand.[23] And, as we've seen, the charged mise-en-scène characteristic of melodrama is what continually modulates the world of affects on the screen; it is what sets the affects flowing.

The house is a privileged space in melodrama. The reason I began this chapter by discussing the domestic spaces in relation to their varying speeds has to do with how these spaces can slow down or speed up the flow of affect. It's almost as if the unchanging decor of the White house tends to freeze affective flow, and thus to solidify the inadequate ideas that dominate the characters. We've seen how Jesse's living quarters are the exception to this law of inertia: Jesse's spaces are in continual flow. They thus bring us—and Jesse—closest to a world of pure affect, one that allows the greatest latitude for action because it is unencumbered by a grid of inadequate ideas.

This world of pure affect is perhaps best realized in the modulations of color that fall across Jesse's face at various moments in the series, motivated by the lights on his oversized stereo system. Color is often thought of as an ideal way to present affect in its sense of "the power to express." One can see this very easily simply by pulling up the color wheel or gradient on a computer screen. We can find a red that expresses the highest power of "redness"; then, as we move the cursor toward the orange shades, we see the power of red diminish as the yellow begins to assert itself, until we arrive at the yellow at its highest power. In the close-ups shown in figures 2.6–2.8 (from the teaser to episode 407 ["Problem Dog"]), various colors wash over Jesse's face, suggesting that he is a kind of blank slate for a number of different potentials that rise up in him. What exactly he is thinking, we are not given to know. (While narratives can always hitch the pure power of color to a number of emotional or mental states, there is no dictionary for assigning content to any given color.) We see only that a series of affective states are cycling through him.

Deleuze notes—and Zarzosa develops this—that the cinematic space proper to the affect-image is the any-space-whatever: the idea being that affects, as virtual potentials, can connect up in an infinite number of ways across space.[24] Jesse's house becomes just such an any-space-whatever, here expressed largely through color that constantly transgresses boundaries. This is most evident in the other shots in the teaser

2.6–2.8. Color as pure affect

2.9. Jesse's house as any-space-whatever

sequence to 407, in which Jesse, while playing the first-person shooter game RAGE, begins hallucinating his real-life shooting of Gale. The walls of Jesse's house, now covered in graffiti from the extended drug parties he has been hosting, get oddly mirrored in the graffiti-covered ruins within the video game, while the glowing colors from the game screen wash over Jesse and emanate throughout the space (fig. 2.9). This is how the any-space-whatever works, by intensification of connections until the point at which the affects link Jesse to a completely different location and time. But this is an immanent engagement with his inner world; thus, if Jesse can be seen as the moral center of the universe of *Breaking Bad*, it is because, of all the characters, he is the one most able to creatively engage with the affective world around him.

While Spinoza was a central reference point for a generation of French intellectuals who came of age in the 1960s, it was Deleuze who ingeniously joined Spinoza's ethics with Nietzsche's devastating critique of morality. I've already hinted at this connection by linking inadequate ideas to "bad interpretations" (for, as Nietzsche famously said, there are no facts, there are only interpretations), and by characterizing happy and sad actions with the creative and the reactive, respectively. I stress this link to Nietzsche because there is a strand of thought that links the moralism of some melodrama to a kind of Nietzschean reactive, or slave, morality (what Nietzsche terms "ressentiment"). This is, for example, how Linda Williams characterizes the contemporary action blockbuster melodrama, where the hero, victimized by the villainous other, stands in for the nation filled with ressentiment, whose suffering renders its actions morally just.[25] One can see how easy it would be to place *Breaking Bad* within this "right cycle" of contemporary popular cultural production and turn *Breaking Bad* into the wish-fulfillment fantasies of the beleaguered and victimized white male of neoliberal American life.[26] But as my discussion of melodrama and mise-en-scène should make clear, while Nietzschean ressentiment is one of the "affective poles" of the series, the series' other affective pole is Nietzschean affirmation and creativity.

How these two poles are to be negotiated is the aesthetic problem of the series, which I will explore in the chapters to follow. In chapter 3, we move from domestic spaces to the object world of contemporary American life, where we will see how objects in the series begin to take on a life of their own, in such a way as to suggest that the creative engagement with the world here is taken up by the camera-eye, so that the aesthetic problem becomes folded into the images themselves.

3 The Puzzle

In the third episode of season one (". . . And the Bag's in the River"), there is a remarkable sequence of events that can serve as an emblem for the ideas to be explored in this chapter (and, indeed, as a kind of key to understanding the way the series makes us inhabit the object world of the early twenty-first century). The background of the sequence is this: In episode 101 ("Pilot"), two low-level neighborhood drug dealers, Emilio and Krazy-8, threaten Walt, believing he is likely a police informer, which leads to Walt concocting a poisonous gas while feigning a meth cook and locking the two in the gas-filled Winnebago. Krazy-8 surprisingly survives the gas, something Walt discovers when through his car windshield he sees the zombie-like Krazy-8 staggering along in the middle of the street (in a shot that is straight out of a contemporary horror film). In episode 103, Krazy-8 has been imprisoned in the basement of Jesse's house, shackled by the neck with a bicycle lock to a support pillar, as Walt agonizes over how he will deal with the situation short of murdering Krazy-8 in cold blood. As he walks down the basement stairs to bring Krazy-8 a sandwich, he has a cancer-induced coughing fit and passes out, dropping the plate with the sandwich on the floor. After he comes to, he sweeps up the pieces of the broken plate, throws them in the garbage, makes another sandwich, and then sits and talks with Krazy-8. Walt eventually becomes convinced that he can avoid killing Krazy-8 and goes upstairs to get the key to the bicycle lock to release Krazy-8 from captivity.

Then begins the sequence of shots I focus on here: Walt moves to the garbage can to throw away an empty beer can, while as he does, the

3.1. The plate

sequence cuts to a seemingly unmotivated close view of the beer can hitting the pieces of the broken plate before the lid closes. But as I've already noted in relation to the way the series constructs itself around indeterminate, or virtual, relations, there is now an inchoate idea hovering in the space, an idea that gradually takes shape as Walt walks away from the garbage can. He then turns around, retrieves the pieces of the broken plate, and starts to reassemble the plate on the kitchen counter. Once the puzzle is put together, he sees that a long, dagger-shaped shard is missing (fig. 3.1). He sees, in other words, *what is not there*, what remains to be actualized within the charged relationship between him and Krazy-8. Just as with the unmotivated cut-away of the garbage can, the editing here throws the viewer into the strange temporal space of the "will-have-been."

The technical procedure organizing the plate scene here is in many ways reminiscent of the films of Alfred Hitchcock. Take, for example, the wine bottles in the cellar in *Notorious* (1946). We discover the secret—that some of the bottles contain uranium ore—only when Dev (Cary Grant) and Alicia (Ingrid Bergman) clumsily knock a bottle of wine to the floor. They clean up the broken glass, but in order to hide the uranium ore powder, they empty a bottle of wine in the sink, fill it with the powder, and then, unable to recork it properly, place the foil around the top to hide the missing cork. Later, the suspicious Sebastian (Claude Rains) will notice, first, that one of the wine bottles is out of place (by its vintage year), then that the foil is covering a missing cork, and finally, the traces of ore and pieces of glass on the cellar floor and the label specifying the year of the broken bottle. Here too, Sebastian learns the truth by way of the trace, or the missing piece of the puzzle.

Hitchcock is justifiably famous for his handling of objects, so that the world and the complex character relationships within it become a vast field of mysteriously charged objects needing to be deciphered. Of all the myriad interpretations of this Hitchcockian procedure, the one most relevant to *Breaking Bad* is that of Gilles Deleuze.[1] Borrowing vocabulary from Charles Peirce, Deleuze argues that the Hitchcockian object world operates via a system of "marks" and "demarks."[2] Groups of interrelated objects can constitute a series grounded by social practices or logical connection. The wine bottle can therefore be at the intersection of any number of series: one series, for example, related to the practice of fine dining, another to collecting and connoisseurship, and so on. Within these series, the bottle remains a mark unless and until something makes it stand out as being out of place. Take, for example, the coffee ritual that is enacted toward the end of *Notorious*, when the doctor visits the house to evaluate Alicia's mysterious debilitating illness. We, the audience, already know that Sebastian and his mother are slowly poisoning Alicia. The initial staging of the scene, with Alicia's coffee cup looming in the foreground as the social ritual transpires behind it, turns the cup into a demark, even though it looks exactly the same as all the other cups. When the doctor accidentally picks up Alicia's cup to take a sip, the panicked overreaction of Sebastian and his mother to what in ordinary circumstances would have been a trivial, absent-minded mistake allows Alicia to see the cup as a demark: she knows she is being poisoned and is helpless to do anything about it.

As is evident in the coffee scene, there is a kind of dark humor in this system: relations of scale are overturned when a gigantic coffee cup dwarfs the humans gathered in the background. This procedure has important connections to surrealist practices, where often the humor and shock effect come from an otherwise ordinary object that has been demarked in some way. Certainly, dark humor is one of the tonal registers that *Breaking Bad* is most noted for; what needs more discussion, however, is its connection to surrealism, and what that can tell us about the aesthetic and political affects that the series produces.

We can begin with simple description. First, there are those iconic images that seem directly indebted to the surrealist archive, that in fact we could imagine at home in a work by Salvador Dalí or Luis Buñuel. Perhaps the most famous is the severed head moving across the desert landscape attached to the back of a large tortoise (207, "Negro y Azul"; fig. 3.2), which then explodes, taking out the group of joking DEA agents who are cavorting around the spectacle. In episode 306 ("Sunset"), when a tribal police officer is checking out a suspicious house, we first learn that the woman who resides there has been murdered when we see her two bare legs on the ground at the corner of the house, crawling with flies (fig. 3.3). Then, as I discussed in chapter 1, there is the murdered boy's hand sticking out from the pile of dirt that covers the rest of him (506, "Buyout"; fig. 1.4). Episode 102 ("Cat's in the Bag . . .") ends with a shot of a young girl absurdly wearing a discarded gas mask as she playfully wanders in the desert (fig. 3.4). And in 308 ("I See You"), there are the disturbing images of Leonel Salamanca in the intensive care unit, his legs having been amputated as a result of a failed attempt to murder Hank: when he recognizes Walter peering in from the door window, he throws himself out of bed and begins crawling like a reptile toward the door, his two stumps leaving smears of blood on the floor (fig. 3.5).

This is far from an exhaustive list of images in the series that present us with a macabre surrealism; suffice to end it with one of my favorites, which occurs in episode 502 ("Madrigal"). It's a long shot of a typical living room arrangement, with the sofa on the back wall flanked on either side by facing armchairs. In the chair at frame right sits Mike Ehrmantraut (having just outsmarted a plot to kill him), while in the other, at frame left, sits the unsuccessful killer. Between the two, in the center of the sofa, sits the corpse of the killer's accomplice, whom the killer has shot in the head a few scenes earlier. The surrealist effect is heightened by having the corpse lean screen left: we know it's a dead body, but as we attend to the dialogue between Mike and the killer, the corpse gives the eerie impression of leaning in to hear the conversation (fig. 3.6). By seeing a dead body in the center of what amounts to a tab-

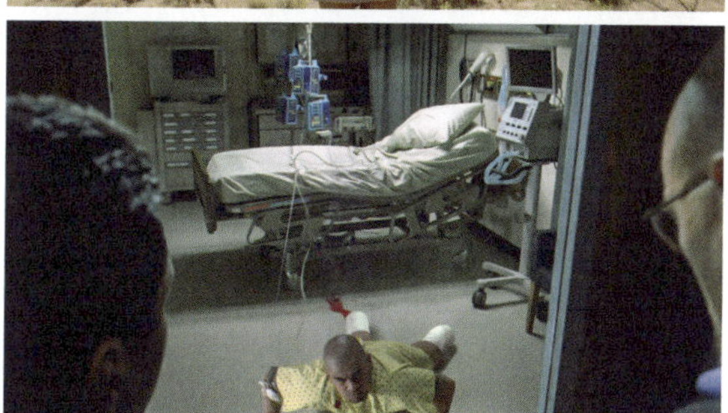

3.2–3.5. Surrealism: Tortuga; legs covered with flies; young girl with gas mask; crawling with stumps

leau of the bourgeois *intérieur*, we might just begin to think of the sterile conformity that underwrites everyday life in consumer society.

But this surrealism becomes a more generalized strategy for presenting what we could call the object world of late capitalism. This is often achieved by bringing objects into unlikely combinations, or by wrenching an object out of its everyday contexts—that is, turning it into a demark—by using it for means far from any of its intended uses. This, for example, makes the images of Krazy-8 in episode 103 so arresting: not simply because the metal bicycle lock has been repurposed, but because once we see it in use as a neck shackle, we begin to think that it might have been expressly invented for that purpose, so neatly does it solve the problem at hand (fig. 3.7). The vicissitudes of crime thus provide the occasion to defamiliarize the everyday world of objects, again often with a wry Hitchcockian, or surrealist, humor. In episode 408 ("Hermanos"), a bewildered Skyler, trying to find a way to hide a huge stash of ill-gotten cash, gets the idea to use the space-saver vacuum bags designed for compressing clothes, only to find that the bags of cash are so heavy that they cause the closet pole to collapse. In 206 ("Peekaboo"), an ATM machine finds its way into the filthy house of a pair of meth addicts (and their neglected five-year-old son). When the husband, trying to crack the machine by tilting it to drill through the bottom, calls his wife a skank, she walks to the machine and nonchalantly tips it forward, crushing her husband's head. The ATM machine responds by suddenly spewing out bills from the cash dispenser, like a slot machine hitting the jackpot in Vegas.

This pushing of the object world toward strangeness underwrites one of the trademark shots of the series, in which the camera is positioned "inside" the object, looking out toward the people in the space—a strategy so prevalent that video essayist Kogonada has made a video homage to the technique.[3] We see Walter's face from inside the tumbling drum of a clothes dryer in which Walt is literally laundering money (101, "Pilot"); we see characters from inside refrigerators, toilets, fireplaces, vending machines, crawl spaces, sinks filled with water, air-conditioning vents, a moving Roomba vacuum cleaner—and, in a send-up, in episode 210 ("Over"), of the "this is your brain on drugs" public service announcement, a shot of Jesse cracking an egg into a hot, clear

3.6. Surrealism: Parlor with corpse

3.7. Repurposing a bicycle lock

frying pan seen from underneath the pan. This stylistic device evokes the idea—so prevalent among the modernists—that things are looking at us, an idea I will return to when I discuss Walter Benjamin's arguments about the political significance of surrealist aesthetics.

When, early in season five, the Vamanos Pest Control company becomes a front for the meth production that is now conducted inside the middle-class houses undergoing treatment for termite infestations, we end up with a brilliantly achieved kind of palimpsest, in which middle-class domesticity is overlaid with drug cooking. On the most obvious level, this places drugs at the center of American middle-class life; at the same time, it indexes a shift from Gus Fring's centralized, Fordist meth lab to a decentralized, just-in-time mode of production more in line with post-Fordism. In episode 503 ("Hazard Play"), we are treated to a montage of a meth cook set to the tune of "On a Clear Day" (very often, the montage set to music provides the series with yet another way to mobilize its black humor, this time via sound-image relations), with a shot that epitomizes the series' surrealist handling of objects. In a cut to the patio, we see brightly colored children's toys spread out as the poisonous gas from the meth production wafts over them (fig. 3.8). In this "Still Life with Poisonous Gas," the sharp registration in the image combined with the distribution of primary colors and the geometric boundaries of the back wall make the image almost worthy of Giorgio de Chirico. While the song's lyrics might initially suggest an ironic evocation of the ecstatic experience of drug use (e.g., "You feel part of every mountain, sea and shore / You can hear from far and near a world you've never heard before"), images like the "de Chirico patio" suggest that the creation of mise-en-scène by the media apparatus can better effect such an expansion of sense perception in a way that not only is less destructive than the drug experience, but that produces a reflective distance necessary for a critical engagement with the present.

When it comes to surrealist treatments of the human figure, these often push the image toward a more obviously postmodern sense of hyperreality, reminiscent of the work of David Lynch. In episodes 103 and 104 ("Cancer Man"), for example, the well-manicured middle-class neighborhood of Jesse's deceased aunt's house (where he lives) is rendered strange by the shots of two elderly women in jogging suits power

3.8. Patio with children's toys and poisonous gas

walking along the side of the street while holding little plastic dumbbells. In 104, this image becomes the prelude to a meth-induced attack of paranoia in Jesse, when he hallucinates that two clean-cut Mormons distributing literature are actually gang members out to murder him. When, in 107 ("A No-Rough-Stuff-Type Deal"), Walt and Jesse go on a mission to steal a barrel of methylamine, rather than wearing the severe black ski masks one is accustomed to seeing in a cinematic heist, they instead wear absurdly bright-colored masks with pom-poms. Later in the same episode, the two are cooking meth in the basement of Jesse's home and are surprised by a realtor holding an open house; the realtor stands in a corner in the kitchen, hiding a can of air freshener behind her while potential buyers are put off by the fumes, and when she notices the coast is clear, she pulls out the air freshener and sprays it around the kitchen in what even she seems to realize is an absurdly ineffective gesture.

Family scenes are often pushed toward a hyperreal absurdity via the point-of-view shot in which the characters being observed stare directly into the camera: for example, Jesse's parents observing him drugged out in the backyard after his attack of paranoia (104; fig. 3.9), or Marie giving an insipid speech to the video camera at the baby shower (107). The most reflexive of these presentations of the family occurs in episode 213

("ABQ"): a television crew has come to do a story on an ideal American family, prompted by the success of Walt Jr.'s website soliciting funds for his father's cancer treatments (only Walt knows that the site is in fact being used to launder money from his drug business), and one long, slightly high-angle shot shows us the entire image-making apparatus. At upper left, we see in the viewfinder of the video camera the White family sitting on the sofa at screen right, while the TV journalist sits in between, "directing" the scene (fig. 3.10).

As I have been suggesting throughout the first chapters of this book, the various strategies of mise-en-scène deployed in the series give it a political edge or attitude, even if such an attitude might cause uneasiness in those who connect political image making to an overtly critical analysis of institutions or systems (as enacted, for example, in *The Wire*). But with our understanding of surrealism as providing an aesthetic tenor for the series, it is useful to consider in some detail the ways in which Walter Benjamin analyzed the political value of the (1920s) movement in his brilliant essay "Surrealism: Last Snapshot of the European Intelligentsia."[4] As many commentators on Benjamin's work have noted, much of his writing, especially during the last decade of his life, was haunted by a sense of political impasse in the wake of the rising tide of fascism throughout Europe. The question then became one of whether and how the arts—the art produced by and for the intelligentsia (surrealism) or the art produced for the masses (cinema)—could productively intervene in this impasse. (And here, we might note that while *Breaking Bad* was produced well before the political events of 2016, the pervasive political polarization in the West, of which those events are symptomatic, was fully in evidence during the series run; while the sense of political impasse has haunted at least some percentage of the Left since the failure of May '68.)

I begin this examination of Benjamin's essay with what is perhaps its most widely known and resonant concept, that of "profane illumination." Surrealist practice finds its objects in the world of the everyday, but it sees within those objects latent energies that their artistic practices could make visible, thus producing in the viewer the sudden affective jolt—the profane illumination—with the potential to reconfigure our relation to the world, and even, Benjamin argues, our sense of self.

3.9. The suburban family

3.10. The media portraying the ideal American family

Benjamin duly notes how this illumination, this ecstatic loosening of the sense of self, also characterizes the drug experience; but he argues (as perhaps does *Breaking Bad*) that the drug experience can only provide us with an "introductory lesson." Of particular interest to the surrealist are the objects (and spaces) that have just recently come to seem dated, superseded by the march of capitalist progress (and its cycles of fashion): these are the objects from which the artist can extract "the revolutionary energies that appear in the 'outmoded.'"[5] It is through this slight temporal gap that history can be politicized, to allow us to see the arbitrariness on which our senses of the good life, and of our entitlement to it, rest. The surrealists, Benjamin argues, "bring the immense forces of 'atmosphere' concealed in these things to the point of explosion."[6]

Benjamin is presenting us here with an effect of *intensity*, exactly in line with my earlier refashioning of the concept of mise-en-scène around the idea of intensive relations. And Benjamin explicitly singles out "the poverty of interiors, enslaved and enslaving objects" as ripe for sudden transformation into "revolutionary nihilism." Here, suffice to recall the shots described earlier of the "parlor conversation with corpse" to see how the surreal positioning of the dead body as interlocutor in the conversation pushes the already dreary shabbiness of the living room toward the funereal, as if middle-class life itself were being embalmed.

Indeed, the poverty of interiors, and enslaved and enslaving objects, has so far been a central focus of this study, as they are a central focus of the series itself. So, to begin with, we might think about why "the outmoded" would be central to surrealist effect. *Breaking Bad*, set solidly in the present, might at first glance seem to challenge this condition of possibility. But the evolution of capitalism since the time of Benjamin's surrealism essay (1929) forces a reconsideration of what, conceptually, "the outmoded" might entail. Late capitalism is characterized not only by increasingly rapid cycles of fashion but also by increasingly rapid technological shifts that interface with the everyday, so that, for example, the clamshell cell phones that are omnipresent in *Breaking Bad* were beginning to become outmoded even before the series ended (the iPhone 4S was introduced in 2011, fully two years before the show's finale). Further, the increasing "weight" of the image archive in postmodern culture leads to an aesthetic of recycling across the cultural field (a central idea in Fredric Jameson's canonical argument about postmodernism),[7] and this aesthetic is fully at work in postmodern interior design. Given these tendencies, no interior, no matter how fashionably up-to-the-minute, can long escape the inexorable slide toward the outmoded, even as its evocations of earlier design moments (e.g., 1950s moderne) can never fully shake off the dust of history despite its current fashionability. If anything, then, the field of the outmoded has vastly expanded since the decades when Benjamin wrote about the glass-and-iron fin de siècle arcades of Paris.

It is in this sense, then, that the interiors and enslaved objects of *Breaking Bad* take on an outmoded quality throughout the series. Consider, for example, the way the series handles the idea of chemistry. When Walter White first meets Gale Boetticher in the superlab, Gale serves him a cup of coffee made from an elaborate contraption put together from flasks, tubing, and assorted other staples of the chemistry lab (fig. 3.11). This image—of the geeky, vaguely asexual Gale displaying his wizardry at putting the "chemistry set" to use for the domestic task of brewing the perfect cup of coffee—might bring to mind in viewers of a certain age the postwar vogue for home chemistry sets, marketed mainly to preadolescent (white) boys, promising to prepare them for the exciting new world ushered in by the petrochemically fueled carbon-chain economy, which would transform domestic life through advances in synthetics, plastics, and pharmaceuticals (the cortisone of *Bigger Than Life* being but one example). "Better Living through Chemistry"—a phrase that in the context of *Breaking Bad* itself produces a dark humor that is akin to its surrealist treatment of objects—was in fact the branding slogan for the DuPont chemical company and could be heard in numerous television ads in the 1950s. There were even, in the 1950s, chemistry sets designed to introduce the budding young scientist to the wonders of atomic energy that came with Geiger counters and radioactive uranium—one of the Gilbert company's atomic sets was numbered U-238! By the end of the 1960s, though, chemistry sets had pretty much vanished from hobby and toy store shelves as a result, some commentators have argued, of both an increasingly vigilant consumer protection appa-

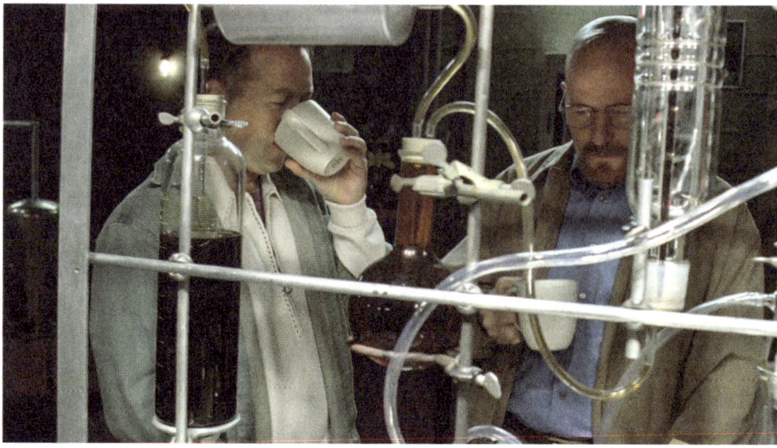

3.11. Gale's "chemistry set"

ratus and—in the wake of thalidomide, pesticides, and Agent Orange—an increasing distrust in the progress narratives put out by the chemical firms (and, indeed, ratified in public discourse as a national project).[8]

In light of this, the images of chemistry paraphernalia throughout the series take on a density as they connect to mental images of outmoded structures of experience: they come to index both an (outmoded) faith in the utopian national project of modernization, and the dark reminders of its potentially lethal consequences. This density then attaches to the ways the series presents meth production, synthesizing the do-it-yourself culture of small-scale meth production with the centralized and mechanized mass production for the cartel, which parallels how the 1950s cultural zeitgeist around chemistry synthesized the pursuit of the hobby with the large-scale production of the chemical companies. This can show us what Benjamin means by the power of the outmoded: the images become untimely, illuminating for us the past that lurks beneath the present, a past in which utopia and disaster are inextricable and whose lethal logic still inhabits the present (here, in the form of "the drug problem"). Two of Benjamin's ideas thus come together: that the image presents us with a hieroglyph, or a puzzle to be deciphered, and that such a deciphering might produce the profane illumination.

The superlab gives us what is perhaps the most reflexive instance of

3.12. The red glow invokes the photographic darkroom

this sense of the outmoded, and not simply because it echoes the Fordist mode of industrial production. Located underneath a large dry-cleaning plant, the subterranean space brings to mind the bomb shelters of the Cold War, while the secret entranceway—underneath an improbably massive dry-cleaning machine that swings away to afford entry—seems like an over-the-top send-up of some secret passageway in a 1960s Roger Corman adaptation of Edgar Allan Poe. (One would think there'd be an easier way to construct a secret entrance!) But what is decisive here is the red: not only are the floors and doors painted a bright red, but—most tellingly—the light at the entrance to the lab glows with the light of a red bulb (fig. 3.12). This red light seems to have nothing to do with the requirements of a meth lab; what it seems more appropriate to—what all the red here seems to be pointing to—is that now outmoded space of the photographic darkroom.

What should be made of this sudden illuminating equation between the photographic apparatus and drugs? Well, to begin with, both initiate a reprogramming of the sensorium. But Benjamin—just like Freud, who realized that psychoanalysis could not be based on the psychically overwhelming recollection of the trauma, but must rather rely on the lengthier processes of repeating and working through to be effective—argues similarly that drugs can only be the first lesson of an illumination that, to be truly effective, must be achieved in full awareness, whether by surrealism or by the "dynamite of the split second" that is the cinema. The series will thus assert the power of the cinematic to illuminate American life in the twenty-first century, and in the process revitalize a way of seeing that (arguably) reached its zenith within the postwar Fordist studio system of classical Hollywood. In the red glow of the photographic darkroom, there is already a way in which the slow appearance of an image as the paper sits in the chemical bath has a haunted quality; in *Breaking Bad*, the spectral eruption of the past within its images extends and intensifies this effect, collapsing past and present in sudden, revelatory shocks. And this is why, for all the protestations Vince Gilligan makes in interviews about how the series should not be seen as celebrating drugs, the series tends to be somewhat sympathetic, not to the profiteers of the drug market, but to the many characters who one way or another fall into the drug scene. Yes, there is tremendous wreckage, but they played a "go for broke" game, the only one imaginable to them, in a social order in which the go-for-broke game is the only one in town.

All of this leads inevitably to the question of politics: both the politics of surrealism as analyzed by Benjamin and the politics of *Breaking Bad*. Benjamin's treatment of the politics of surrealism is dense and allusive, and as complex as was the movement's own relationship to politics. In the first place, the seemingly anarchic energies the surrealists brought to bear on the everyday might seem to some to be counterproductive to the kind of revolutionary political activity that could lead to actual results in the real world. But the surrealists, Benjamin argues, were onto something that the "well-meaning left-wing bourgeois intelligentsia" (his phrase) could not see.[9] Both the surrealists (through their work) and Benjamin (through his analytical acumen) criticize this strand of left-wing thinking as being hopelessly enmeshed in idealist morality. The result is that the hoariest conservative ideals—metaphors which as Benjamin describes them bear a remarkable affinity to the contemporary metaphors of the family and the future that Lee Edelman so devastatingly critiqued via the concept of "reproductive futurism" in his book *No Future*[10]—are trotted out to "ground" the desire for revolution, without any awareness that these very ideals are part of the superstructure that holds the repressive present together in the first place! And in a curious line toward the end of the essay, Benjamin paraphrases Trotsky's idea that we won't know what a revolutionary artist looks like until after a revolution has been achieved. From the vantage point of this study, we could summarize the argument this way: the error of Benjamin's "well-meaning left" is that it imposes on the political a *transcendental* frame of reference so as to control how the future will unfold, whereas the surrealist, like the revolutionary, acts within a field of pure *immanence*, in which the very frames of reference by which things have heretofore been judged are now up for grabs.

Benjamin's position here is grounded in the very real, very material transformations that modernity had wrought across the social space. As opposed to the space of metaphor that had grounded the politics of the past in discursive structures, the masses of the early twentieth century live and move within an "image-space" and a "body-space," both of which are continually calibrated one to the other via new technologies such as the cinema.[11] Today, of course, video games are the newest technology to perform this calibration of image- and body-space. We might then return to the scene, discussed in chapter 2, in which Jesse plays a first-person shooter game while recollecting the killing of Gale (407, "Problem Dog"; fig. 2.9). Here, the graffiti-covered walls of his neglected home begin to mirror the image-space of the video game, while Jesse's bodily movements reenact a traumatic past moment. Thus instead of connecting him to the prevailing metaphors of the military-entertainment complex, the video game ends up connecting Jesse affectively to his own experience, his own present life.

Benjamin will later argue that perception itself, far from being a hard-wired human universal, is instead conditioned by history.[12] In the surrealism essay, though, he seems to suggest that, with the advent of modernity and its attendant technologies of the image, our resulting "expanded" perception (our image-space and body-space) no longer seamlessly coincides with the reigning metaphors organizing our lives. The political problem then becomes how we move from individual to collective; in an admittedly dense passage in the essay, Benjamin writes, "Only when in technology body and image space so interpenetrate that all revolutionary tension becomes bodily collective innervation, and all the bodily innervations of the collective become revolutionary discharge, has reality transcended itself to the extent demanded by the *Communist Manifesto*. For the moment, only the Surrealists have understood its present commands."[13] While what, exactly, Benjamin meant by "collective innervation" as a path toward revolutionary action remained obscure in his work,[14] his understanding of surrealist practice as reconfiguring body- and image-spaces is astute. And these interventions, these attempts to alter our fundamental sense of being in the world, are strictly immanent to that world. In a certain sense, we could say that Benjamin sees surrealist practice as opening up a kind of clearing ground on which something new (and ideally, something liberatory) can be built; but what that something will look like cannot be given in advance.

Admittedly, the twenty-first-century world of *Breaking Bad* is far from the modernist Europe of Benjamin and the surrealists; as a concept, "the masses" no longer makes sense in advanced consumer capitalism, and collectivity has given way to dispersed networks of information flows. But in its construction of surrealist imagery, *Breaking Bad* exemplifies Benjamin's observation that surrealism is a practice that operates immanently, outside a pregiven or transcendental frame of reference. This is why the politics of the series has been the subject of so much argument. (For example, the series has been criticized at the level of its representations of the ethnic other, but to do this is to impose a preordained representationalist frame to one's aesthetic evaluation.)

In the introduction to this book, I mobilized Robert Ray's notion of left and right cycles in relation to contemporary quality television and argued that *The Wire* and *Breaking Bad* were the prime examples of the two tendencies, respectively. Now I can add more nuance to this characterization: *The Wire*, with its fundamental concern with structures and institutions, imposes a transcendental frame on its material, if only by way of the overarching foci of the various seasons. This is its tie to the late nineteenth-century aesthetic of naturalism, and some of the criticisms made of naturalism can carry over to that series. *Breaking Bad* gives us no such overarching frames of reference, but rather presents us with situations and events in their (immanent) unfoldings. The focus on the situation as it unfolds pushes the series toward an improvisational logic, in terms of both narrative and mise-en-scène. At the level of narrative, this improvisational logic connects the series to one of its key sources, the spaghetti western (which I will take up in chapter 4). At the level of mise-en-scène, however, this is a logic through which we try to extract the maximum pressure from all the elements of the scene that are at hand. The surrealist image is but one of any number of these extractions. Now, it is precisely this disconnection of the affective from its explanatory frames that, politically, makes the series seem to some to be cynical and nihilistic (and therefore partaking of the right cycle in contemporary television), just as the surrealists themselves were subjected to the charge of nihilism and, ultimately, conservatism. But in line with Benjamin's defense of surrealism, is there a way to see the aesthetic maneuvers of *Breaking Bad* as vital to a progressive politics for our own age? The question might be rephrased thusly: How does the series' reveling in improvisatory play allow us to imagine reconfigurations of our image-spaces, our body-spaces, and the technologies that calibrate the two?

We can explore this via the "magnet" plot in episode 501 ("Live Free or Die"). Here we get a kind of "motivation of the device," insofar as the wildly incongruous juxtaposition of objects is produced by a giant magnet that Walter and Jesse rig up in order to wipe the hard drive of the just-murdered Gus Fring, whose laptop contains surveillance footage of Walter and Jesse cooking meth in the superlab. As they attempt to concoct a magnet powerful enough to penetrate the walls of the evidence pound, the episode once again throws us into an auto graveyard and into the DIY culture the series tends to celebrate, as the men rig up the giant electromagnet used for moving junk cars to a bunch of car batteries. The actual caper at the police headquarters is shown with standard crosscutting between Walt and Jesse cranking up the power of the magnet and the interior of the evidence storage room; but this interior is given to us initially via a series of close-ups of objects in the room, including a lowly metal paper clip that we see begin to move across the desk as the magnetic field intensity increases. This begins a wild orchestration of an object-world gone completely topsy-turvy, as the metal lamps begin to hang at an angle skewed from the vertical, the metal shelving units begin to cascade into one another like dominoes, and, ultimately, the

3.13. Magnet: The archive of evidence is scrambled

metal objects in the room are plastered together in a kind of surrealist collage along the wall (fig. 3.13).

Here, the very archive of evidence that permits us to adjudicate a case (guilty or innocent? good or bad?) is thrown into chaos. On one level, we could take this as a direct illustration of the way that technology might intervene to recalibrate the relationships between bodies and images. What is the relationship between a laptop and a paper clip? Why are shelving units made of metal? Does the police department order them from Walmart? Yet there is a deeper allegory at work here, for who today has not needed to wipe a hard drive, or has not regretted having improperly disposed of an old computer? And who hasn't worried at some point or other about how much information "they" have on us? But what we are given in this wild celebration of the pure possibilities of the cinematic is a political affect that cuts across standard American left-right narratives: these might be the worries of both supporters of Edward Snowden and Julian Assange, and right-wing survivalist militia groups. In this sense, we are given the political affect outside of its current, explanatory narratives, with the suggestion that perhaps some new and unimagined space might be opened up for understanding life in the twenty-first century.

Through a Glass Darkly

One of *Breaking Bad*'s recurring strategies is to begin the sequence with a partial or ambiguous view; we don't quite know what we are looking at, or where we are moving, until the shots slowly allow the mystery to unfold.[15] This is done at a macro level in some of the cold openings: for example (as discussed in chapter 1), the mysterious footage of the pink teddy bear and accident scene that becomes clarified only when we see the plane crash in the finale of season two (213). But this strategy is very often used at the micro level of the stand-alone sequence, where we are presented with an image of an object or a partial view of a scene (as in the skull-capped boots of the Salamanca brothers exiting a Mercedes in episode 301 ["No Más"]), opening up to a still unclear action (the impeccably suited brothers drop to the ground and begin crawling like lizards with a crowd of peasants), until a shot finally allows us to assign meaning to what we've seen (the shrine of Santa Muerte, where the brothers place a picture of "Heisenberg" on the small altar). This formal strategy extends the idea of the world as a puzzle to be deciphered by foregrounding the role of our own interpretive processes in understanding images.

We can see a similar idea at work in the cinematography: the lighting and camera positioning—so indebted to film noir and to cinematographer Gordon Willis's rethinking of the noir aesthetic for color film stock in *The Godfather*—often tends to hide as much as it shows. We often find ourselves in rooms whose corners are plunged into darkness or obscurity; light sources will produce hot spots in the image, as if the light itself must struggle to illuminate an all-engulfing darkness. This system of lighting occurs so often that it would be a rather pointless exercise to enumerate every instance. I noted in chapter 2 how the various parts of the White house—for example, the bedroom at night, invaded by the beams of car headlights—are lit in this noir-like way, but the lighting idea can manifest itself in practically any interior. It's especially evident as we move toward the more extreme manifestations of the wreckage of addiction: the house of the meth heads with the young boy and the stolen ATM machine; the seedy room of the meth hotel where Jesse holes up with Wendy; the shooting gallery in 213 where Walter searches for the drugged-out Jesse, who is inconsolable after the death of Jane. This last sequence presents us with a triumph of mise-en-scène, insofar as the images adopt the position of the outsider crossing the threshold into an alien world, the threshold itself highlighted by the interior darkness that engulfs the frame on either side of the doorway (fig. 3.14). Whether or not the production team was thinking here of John Ford's *The Searchers* (1956), I cannot say, but as Walt walks through the space in search of a Jesse who "doesn't belong there," the sequence cannot help but resonate with that iconic moment in the evolution of the western when Ethan Edwards (John Wayne) enters the tribal compound in search of his niece.

But the dark lighting isn't reserved only for the derelict spaces of drug addicts: it becomes the principal lighting idea of the series, as the chemical world of drugs encroaches more and more on every aspect of everyone's lives. By the time we get to the teaser of 509 ("Blood Money"), the White house has come to resemble nothing less than the shooting gallery of 213, with the boarded-up windows producing narrow shafts of sunlight that cut through the abandoned, rotting house, barely making readable the graffiti spelling out "Heisenberg" on one wall (fig. 3.15). What was once the alien world has now taken over the familiar, and we understand it differently now, as logically connected to the world we know. By the second half of the final season, the darkness has seemingly taken control of the world. If the exterior landscapes once partook of the majestic openness of the Monument Valley so beloved of John Ford and Sergio Leone, as if inspiring the pioneer to think, "I can create something here," by the final half season the sun seems to be sinking toward the horizon, casting strangely long shadows across the earth, or else it seems to be beating down with such ferocity that the earth has turned into a barren wasteland. In episode 510 ("Buried"), Walter goes out to the desert to bury the barrels of cash he had stored in a rental space, and the low sun hovering just above a mountain top burns in the image (fig. 3.16), until it gives way to magic hour and then the absolute darkness of the desert, illuminated only by the lights of the van. It's as if a metaphysics of "the dark sun"—always threatening in the series—has finally taken full hold.

A related motif within the images of *Breaking Bad* is the quality of

3.14. Echoes of *The Searchers* in the meth house

3.15. The White house finally resembles a drug house

3.16. The sun burns the image

fragmentation, even frangibility, that they present to us. Shots are often constructed with multiple planes, each plane giving a fragment or piece of the entire scene. For example, in the shot from 102 when Walter sees the zombified Krazy-8 staggering in the street, the image is constructed around at least four planes: Walt's hand on the steering wheel in foreground left, Krazy-8 in the background right, the visible plane of the windshield separating them, and then Walt's eyes taking in the scene in the car's rearview mirror (fig. 3.17). The idea comes together from the various pieces within the frame. Often, the image becomes so brittle that it breaks into many pieces, sometimes motivated by surfaces like broken windshields. We could say that the crystal meth production, which ends when a glassy sheet of meth is cracked into pieces for distribution, is what motivates this device in the mise-en-scène, as if the entire world is slowly becoming crystalline. One of the most stunning examples of this is a black-and-white shot in the teaser to episode 213, in which the camera looks out through the cracked windshield of Walt's car at an approaching man in a hazmat suit, and as the camera moves rightward across the cracked windshield, the changing focal plane produces dozens of shimmering hexagonal flares across the screen, and the image seems to be crystallizing before our eyes (fig. 3.18).

3.17. Image fragmented into four planes

3.18. The world becoming crystalline

Deleuze famously theorized that the transition from the classical cinema of movement and action to the modern cinema of time and thought was heralded by the emergence of a new kind of image, the "crystal image." To put it in the simplest possible terms, the crystal image forms when an image of something actual interacts with its virtual counterpart (say, its mirror reflection) to the point where the actual and the virtual become, in his words, "indiscernable."[16] The image and its virtual counterpart can be literally shown on the screen, as in the many instances in the series where we see characters reflected in windows, windshields, mirrors, and other surfaces. But the actual and virtual can enter into relation in the image in less direct ways: in, for example, the exchange between the shattered windshield and the light rays streaming through it, such that the visible and the invisible enter into a relationship in which something new erupts into the image. Once the actual and virtual begin interacting in this way, a number of consequences ensue. In the first place, instead of the virtual producing a concrete "local" reaction to a given situation, we now get actions-at-a-distance, where a virtual potential over here leads to some seemingly unconnected event over there. We've seen in chapter 1 how the elliptical editing of *Breaking Bad* produces just such effects of actions-at-a-distance, outside the normal chain of cause and effect that governs classical cinema.

Yet another aspect of the crystalline regime is the appearance of forking in the narrative: the story will fork in unexpected directions, like a crystal growing in a solution, as the various potential energies within the world get actualized one by one, so that the part and the whole enter into a new kind of interdependence. We've already seen how the teasers scramble the linearity of the narrative line, producing forks that recall past events or anticipate future ones, setting in motion a virtual world that hovers insistently over the present. And in chapter 4, we will see how the gamelike and improvisatory logic of many key sequences introduces sudden, unexpected forks in the narrative line. Ultimately, Deleuze sees the crystal image as putting "the truth in crisis," and so bringing into being "the powers of the false."[17] *Citizen Kane* (Orson Welles, 1941) is a good illustration of this: each story we are given is a partial account of the events of Kane's life, but the stories alternately reinforce and contradict one another, and we never arrive at "the truth" about Kane.

But there is a more fundamental question lurking beneath the invocation of Deleuze here: namely, is it even possible for television to produce the crystalline regime that Deleuze sees in postclassical cinema? To this, I would say yes: and that television can produce this regime in a more expansive way than cinema does, precisely because of the particular ways that television inhabits our lives (and we inhabit television) over the long run. The crystalline regime now is no longer experienced as a discrete, cinematic event, but rather becomes something that is lived over time, as we keep returning to places that are "the same, but different," places that themselves are contiguous to the spaces in which our own lives unfold. Slowly, our programmed, habitual responses to the world can be "jammed" by the crystal, and we will be led to a perception beyond the human: a perception of what Deleuze called "non-organic Life," or in Jane Bennet's words, of "vibrant matter."[18]

Finally, we can note the ways that the human body gets caught up in the fractured play of reflective surfaces throughout the series. On one level, this is but another result of the noir lighting and composition. Bodies and faces are routinely broken up by mirrors and other reflective surfaces (as we saw in the shot where Walter, driving, spots Krazy-8 in the street), while the shadows cast by bodies sometimes become strong compositional elements of the frame. In episode 104, when Jesse has a meth-induced attack of paranoia and hallucinates that Mormon missionaries are members of a biker gang out to kill him, we see him in tight close-up peering from behind glass, with the bars and curlicues of the worn wrought iron cutting across his face, while the chintzy voile patterned curtain hides his face from the upper lip down. Sometimes the camera alone is able to make the body seem as if refracted through a medium, as in episode 312 ("Half Measures"), when we see Jesse preparing to confront the murderers of the kid Tomás, his face reflected in the compact disc from which he will snort crystal, then smearing across the screen and reconstituting itself, making us unsure whether we're seeing the face or its reflection (fig. 3.19). This smearing of the face also occurs in episode 413 ("Face Off"), when Gus Fring screams just before the bomb is going to go off (fig. 3.20); here, the image achieves a presentation of pure affect that resembles the effect Francis Bacon achieves in his paintings of the screaming popes. Yet another stunning example of facial refraction occurs in 509, where Walt's glasses seem to smear across his brow, while at frame left octagonal flares of light shimmer in the blackness (fig. 3.21).

This concern with the reflected body throughout the series suggests that we are looking at things "through a glass, darkly," that underneath the mundane world of appearances there lies another world, parallel to our own, but uncanny and strange. On one level, of course, this may be seen as a reprise of the way film noir divides the world into the brightness of "normalcy" and the darkness of the underworld, the mundane high school classroom and the violent yet alluring drug trade. But *Breaking Bad* extends our understanding of this aesthetic device beyond its connection to noir. In episode 102, Walter gives a lecture to his class on the concept of the chiral molecule (a topic that seems pretty advanced for a high school chemistry class). As he explains it, holding up his hands to illustrate, two molecules have a chiral relationship when one of them is the mirror image of the other (fig. 3.22). This announces that there is a fundamental rift in the creation—at the level of molecules—such that they will divide into left-handed and right-handed versions, mirror images, but not identical. Walter, although distracted by his recent murder of Emilio (and, so he thinks, Krazy-8), comes up with the example of thalidomide: one molecule is a wonder drug that eases the distress of morning sickness in pregnant women, while its chiral counterpart produces monstrous deformities in the fetus. On the one hand, there is the faith in scientific progress that ensures the smoothest possible reproduction of the nuclear family, and on the other hand, there is the nightmare of science producing "mutant" children.

Here, we might note that since the postwar modernizations, there have been recurring cycles in the SF-horror genre in which something—usually new technology, but maybe just the television set itself—has turned the younger generation into a generation of monsters, capable of murderous rage or extrahuman powers. In the postwar boom years alone, we have Mervyn LeRoy's *The Bad Seed* (1956), Joseph Losey's *These Are the Damned* (1962), and a number of others. Stanley Kubrick,

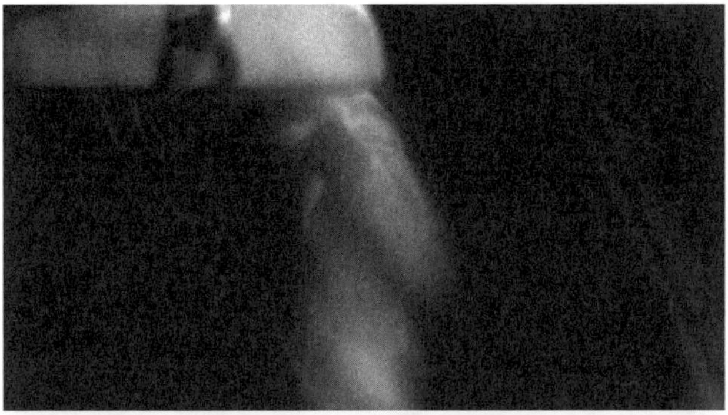

3.19 and **3.20**. Close-up: Capturing affect

3.21. Refractive effects in the image

3.22. “Chiral”

with *The Shining* (1980), brilliantly upended the formula, turning the patriarchal father into a terrorizing monster, with the possibly abused son possessed of the gift of telepathy that will save him and his mother from the tyranny of Logos itself, the typewriter that keeps churning out the same cliché over and over again. Here, chirality—in the form of the eerie signifier “REDRUM” (with an inverted *D* and *R*)—is the hinge or pivot between the actual world and its virtual (“shining”) counterpart (fig. 3.23). The idea of chirality breaks through the Manichean duality we connect to noir, in favor of a more generalized exchange between actual and virtual that, as I noted earlier, is a generator of the crystal image: the chiral gives us the indistinguishable circuit between the two.

Thus, when the body fragments or multiplies in the image, even though this procedure finds its roots in postwar film noir (and before that, in German expressionism), it connects in *Breaking Bad* to a fundamentally different conception of the individual, one that emerged only after the end of modernity. Expressionism and, later, noir adhere to a Freudian view of the individual whereby the seemingly rational conscious mind is driven by repressed, unconscious, and transgressive desires and fantasies; it presents us with a dualism of the psyche that then gets projected into the geography of the city, where underneath the rational order of office towers and regulated traffic flows there lurks the

3.23. *The Shining* (Stanley Kubrick, 1980): Exchange between actual and virtual

dark underground of subway tubes, smoky basement jazz clubs, dark alleyways that lead nowhere.

Perhaps Gus Fring is the character that most exemplifies the dualism of the noir subject (though I will qualify this in chapter 4). This is largely because of his death scene, where, in another one of those cinematic hauntings that grace the series, in his death he is likened to Debby Marsh (Gloria Grahame) in Fritz Lang's *The Big Heat* (1953). (While it may be that this connection has been made somewhere in the vast commentary by critics and fans of the show, I have not run into it.) In Lang's film, Debby is the "B-girl" who hangs out with mobsters; after her boyfriend Vince Stone (Lee Marvin) throws a pot of scalding coffee in her face, she goes through the rest of the film with one side of her face bandaged and disfigured, while the other side retains its exquisite beauty (fig. 3.24). She then befriends detective Dave Bannion (Glenn Ford) and decides to abandon her criminal friends. At one point, she positions herself in Bannion's flophouse room with her "bad side" turned away, so that she can present her "good side" to Bannion. In the shot in which Gus Fring emerges from the room where the old Salamanca has set off the bomb—a shot celebrated enough to have been given its own "behind-the-scenes" extra in the box set of the series—we see Fring in profile from a camera positioned down the corridor, seemingly un-

3.24. Gloria Grahame in *The Big Heat* (Fritz Lang, 1953): Good side/bad side

harmed by the blast as he stands straightening his tie. But as the staff of the old folks' home rush from the other end of the corridor toward the site of the explosion and the figure of Fring, they see him from the other side, the camera registering the shocked looks on their faces. Then the camera begins its move toward a frontal view of Fring, and we see that the other half of his face has been blown up.

Gus Fring can be treated in this dualistic manner because he is the closest to a figure of "radical evil" in the series: for him, all of human life is only a matter for his own calculus. He is the great, cold calculator of the series, to the point where he seems telepathic—as when he senses in episode 412 ("End Times") that a bomb might have been planted in his car and thus foils Walter's first attempt to kill him. Consider the elaborate scheme he concocts to poison all the members of Eladio's cartel in Mexico (410, "Salud"), which entails his drinking and then vomiting up the poisoned tequila he presents as a rare gift. Even if Walter White discovers within himself a great power to maneuver himself out of situations of grave danger, this maneuvering always seems so much ad hoc

3.25. Walt's multiple reflections

improvisation, which is why his actions appear "all over the place," never having the consistency that we see in Fring.

We could say that Walt lives up to his "namesake," Walt Whitman: he contains multitudes. Thus, often, when we are presented with a noir image of Walter, we get not one shadowy Other, but rather multiple others: in a shot of Walt in his classroom in 207 ("Negro y Azul"), he is reflected by the painted skeleton behind him, while his shadows multiply on the uneven wall next to it (fig. 3.25). This is not to say that Walter's shadows and reflections are *always* fragmented in this way. In fact, the series is punctuated with many images in which Walter is doubled by his reflection. However, it is unsatisfying to think of these reflections in terms of the simple dualism of "Mr. Chips or Scarface." Rather, like the crystal, these images have a multiplier effect: this or that, or that, or that, or that . . .

This shift—from the divided self of modernity to the multiplied self of today—is the corollary to a larger social, economic, and cultural shift as neoliberal regimes of accumulation supplant the earlier organization of mass production and consumption in the advanced economies. We can boil this down to how we are to understand the very idea of "calculability." The Freudian unconscious in a sense localized the zone of incalculability in the dream, the slip-up, the symptom. While this still

3.26. The constellation

holds, we more and more find ourselves within a greatly expanded field of incalculabilities built into the very structure of neoliberal capitalism. To turn for a moment to my discussion, in chapter 1, of the disruption of cause-effect logic in the series, we can begin now to see how it is connected, not simply to traditions of art cinema as aesthetic sources, but more deeply to some fundamental shift in the structures of everyday life.

In this chapter, I've attempted to understand in a deep sense the aesthetics of the image in *Breaking Bad*. I'd like to end by looking at what I take to be a very special image, which may provide a vantage point from which to think about all the other images. This is the view from inside the Los Pollos Hermanos truck after would-be hijackers have riven the side of the truck with bullets from automatic weapons. Like a starry night, the bullet holes appear to form a constellation within the blackness of the truck's interior (fig. 3.26). For Walter Benjamin (as also for his Frankfurt School colleagues Siegfried Kracauer and Theodor Adorno), the constellation had a conceptual value of considerable importance. The individual stars in a given constellation do not have a necessary connection to one another in the physical universe: the constellation is rather the imaginative move, by humans, through which elements in an unrelated group are made to interconnect, in such a way as to allow us to navigate the world. But the constellation also has another, more revelatory power: as in astrology, the power to connect the distant past with the promise of a future life. So might not the profane illuminations of the surrealists (or of the cinematic apparatus) perhaps produce new constellations of meaning out of the scrapheap of industrial modernity, to thus usher in new arrangements of things and so "redeem" the brutal history that has brought us to the present?

The constellation thus gives us an image for a strictly immanent engagement with the world, in keeping with the working methods of Benjamin and Kracauer, who scoured the surfaces of the modern world, putting together the fragments in order to attempt to think a politics that emerges immanently from our experience of that world. I will thus take this image from *Breaking Bad*—one that repeats in several other episodes of the series—to be tutelary: it alerts us to the fact that we have been given the pieces of the puzzle, but also that out of those pieces something vital and liberatory may emerge.

4 Just Gaming

By episode 404 ("Bullet Points"), Skyler has crossed a crucial threshold: she will now become an active accomplice in laundering the money from Walt's drug cooking through the car wash—the very same car wash that in episode 101 was the site of Walt's humiliation and degraded masculinity—that she has been instrumental in buying and which she will now manage. "Tonight's the night, no turning back," she says as she lays out a round of blackjack on the table. In order to explain to Hank and Marie how they are suddenly able to buy the business (and, to Marie, how they have been able to pay for Hank's expensive physical therapy, which he wrongly thinks is covered by his insurance), Skyler has concocted the narrative that Walt began recklessly, but successfully, gambling after his cancer diagnosis; that he found himself to be adept at counting cards in blackjack, allowing him to win a small fortune; that all of his mysterious comings and goings that seemed so suspicious to Marie and that had caused Skyler to file for divorce—the second cell phone, the fugue state—were actually covers not for his meth cooking, but rather for the gambling addiction that he has now become ashamed of and is in treatment for. What follows is a hilarious set piece—a "beat" running for over nine minutes—in which Skyler makes Walt rehearse with her the script she's written to make their story as convincing as possible.

Of course, on one level, the scene is reflexive, showing us the process by which any of the dramatic scenes in the series might have been rehearsed; on another level, it's highly ironic in that Skyler has finally managed, with the dismal scenario she's concocted, to engage her talent for creative writing. With scripts in hand, Skyler begins the rehearsal with the announcement of "the exciting news" that they are buying a car wash, an event for which Hank and Marie are sure to ask how they could afford it; at this point, Skyler will come in with the lines—reading from her script now—"We want to tell you the whole story . . . it's a doozy . . . so hold on to your hats!" We have to laugh at the conviction with which Skyler delivers her cliché-ridden dialogue while Walt, slumped in a chair, stares at her in disbelief. "It accomplishes two things," Skyler explains: "it keeps it light while letting them know to expect something big"—to which Walt replies sardonically, "Yeah. It's a doozy." As the rehearsal continues, Walt protests the weak position the script puts him in, saying he doesn't want to look bad in front of his son. The rehearsal ends with Skyler practicing her final lines, suggesting that she might then have a tear run down her cheek. When we finally see the performance in the next scene, we see only Skyler delivering those final lines, complete with the tear. But the result of the performance is an amazed Hank with a newfound respect for his brother-in-law, while Junior looks at his father in admiration and says, "Dad, you're a stud!" Here, we see how the scenario they concocted transfers their legitimate guilt over Walt's drug activities onto the relatively more "innocent" activity of gambling.

Skyler and Walt's scenario in 404, however, is nothing compared with the "doozy" they record on DVD in episode 511 ("Confessions"). By this time, Hank and Marie know that Walt is the notorious meth cook Heisenberg, but Hank doesn't have enough yet to bring charges to the DEA. In a tense meeting at a taqueria, Walt gives Hank a DVD of his "confession," and in the next scene, we see Hank and Marie standing in the living room, watching aghast as the recorded Walt renarrates the entire story we've seen unfold across five seasons so that Hank is pegged as the master criminal Heisenberg. The made-up tale is perfectly plausible within the genre of the "rogue cop" film, the premise here being that Hank is the one who broke bad, teaming up with the criminal Gus Fring. The new story cunningly spins key narrative elements—Gus having ordered a hit on Hank, Hank's rehabilitation from the attempted hit paid for by drug money—into completely believable events in an alternate narrative universe. In other words, the same events take on entirely different meanings when they move from the genre of the melodrama of the mild-mannered school teacher stumbling into the world of the streets to the genre of the cop who goes rogue, lured by the temptations of the underworld: the genre conventions guide us in our interpretation in both cases.

These "meta" scenes are important insofar as they show us the elements of play that are involved in the creation of narrative.[1] The writers' rooms of television series generally contain something along the lines of a corkboard with cards, each representing another imaginative move in the narrative game, and expanses of empty beige cork representing the holes in the story that need to be filled in. But while these particular scenes are special insofar as they foreground for us the machinery that leads to the production of the story, more important for our analysis is that *Breaking Bad* takes this gamelike approach to narrative as a general principle: almost every event plays itself out in relation to moves and countermoves, with deep implications for our understanding of contemporary media and its relation to the everyday life of the neoliberal subject, hinted at in our discussion in chapter 3 of the fragmentation of the contemporary subject in relation to incalculable futures.

By now, it has become a cliché of critical theory that our postmodern age is characterized by the loss of the "master narrative." We no longer, for example, have a (near) universally shared idea of what constitutes "the American project"; instead—and to a great extent because of a vastly expanded dissemination of images and information in the mediasphere—we get a proliferation of disparate groupings adhering to seemingly incompatible versions of the national project (with the resulting political paralysis that is evident in U.S. politics as I write). There is still a generalized adherence to some overarching idea of America, but it is as if scraps or fragments of the idea get taken up and woven into genres as different as the conspiracy narrative, the self-actualization narrative, the immigration narrative, and on and on; and the rules governing how we understand one another, governing communication and discourse, change when we move from one genre to the other, from one micropolitical "tribe" to another.

When the neophyte meth cook Walter White first attempts to distribute his product, he's still ensconced within the discourse community of the white, suburban, low-paid professional class of middle America, while the Latino drug dealer Krazy-8—with his pit bull, punching bag, nickname, and cousin just bailed out from a prison stint—moves in a completely different world, one in which the solution to the situation in which they find themselves in episode 103 (". . . And the Bag's in the River"), with Krazy-8 imprisoned in Jesse's basement, would seem to lie not in any kind of negotiation, but in a fight to the death. But Walter is not cut out—at least, so it seems—for the latter, so he desperately seeks a way to make the two worlds, the two discourse communities, come together via some sort of compromise or consensus. He shares with Krazy-8 his recent cancer diagnosis (which he still hasn't shared with his family), while Krazy-8 tells Walter about his father's local furniture business, with its tacky, low-budget TV commercials. Walter then recalls that they still have the crib they bought years ago from Krazy-8's father's store for the birth of their son. Might not these familial interconnections be able to bring the two worlds together? But at this early point in the story, neither Walt nor we the audience understand that the family—and the reproductive futurism that underwrites it—is an "inadequate idea" in the way I developed this notion in chapter 2. When Walt pieces together the broken plate and discovers the missing shard, he realizes that despite the seeming connection, he and Krazy-8 are playing two different language games, and that the rules governing one game are totally incompatible with those governing the other.

The notion that—in the age of information proliferation that we call postmodernity—"global" master narratives have splintered into various competing "local" narratives, each with its own rules governing interpretation and thus each representing a different language game, was put forward most notably by French philosopher Jean-François Lyotard. In some works, like *Just Gaming*, he characterized this development as akin to paganism, for paganism too posits a multiplicity of local explanatory narratives rather than one, overarching master narrative to explain the world.[2] In *The Postmodern Condition*, Lyotard links this proliferation of local knowledges and narratives to the dramatic rise in information technologies.[3] But what became the critical philosophical problem for Lyotard is the question of how to make a judgment of truth that can have currency beyond the merely local, or how to adjudicate an ethical claim that cuts across two or more different localized "tribes."

To bring to bear on this question some of the concepts set forth in chapter 3, we could begin by saying that, insofar as Lyotard's model of communication is true, then any model to adjudicate the truth or the justice in a situation (or, more precisely in Lyotard's philosophy, in an "event") must be immanent to the situation and the players involved; we cannot resort to a preordained, transcendental frame or ground from which to make the judgment, for that would turn one narrative into the master narrative that has been irrevocably lost.[4] This is why the concept of breaking bad achieves such resonance: the "bad" in the phrase conjures some transcendental criterion to distinguish the good from the bad, once and for all; but the "breaking"—a verb in the gerund form—suggests a process that is first and foremost a becoming, enmeshed in the immanent particularities of an event that is unfolding, an event whose "goodness" or "badness" has yet to be determined. As we've seen in earlier chapters, *Breaking Bad*'s aesthetic strategies as a general rule emphasize the "breaking" over the "bad," the cinematic being how we characterize those strategies that start with the immanent givens of the space and then push the latent energies therein to maximum expression.

Contemporary philosophers like Lyotard and Gilles Deleuze propose an ontology of the event (rather than an ontology of the object); instead of the fixity of objects and properties, we have the singularities of events, no two of which will ever be exactly the same. Such a philosophy will emphasize forces, affects, and becomings; every event, in its singularity or uniqueness, will necessarily exceed any interpretive frame that attempts to assign it meaning once and for all. *Breaking Bad* forces us to look at the world through this "logic of the event": its aesthetic procedures (the narrative indetermination, the unfolding of forces in the mise-en-scène, the spectral resonances with classical cinema, the eruptions of surrealism and noir, the search for an "adequate idea") push us toward this logic of the singular event.

This has far-reaching implications for television studies, because it has been argued that television, as an apparatus, most fully realizes itself in the face of the singular event of catastrophe:[5] from the assassination of JFK to the falling of the World Trade Center, television becomes the unifying relay between us and the event as it unfolds. However, in the face of these "eruptions of the Real," television's principal goal is to provide the catastrophic event with a master narrative that will explain it; indeed, this is an instance of that "artifactuality," or manufacture of the present, that Jacques Derrida and Bernard Stiegler think is the crucial function of television.[6] But what I've identified as the cinematic can actually draw on the power of televisual seriality to hold the event open and indeterminate, and to extend this experience of indetermination over longer and longer periods of time, in such a way that we may begin to see the world much more provisionally, as a series of events whose interpretations we must *work* to attain. Such has been my argument to this point. In this chapter, I will explore how the improvisation and game playing that ensue from an ontology of the event are enacted in the series; how these "just-in-time" performances of the self are expressive of much deeper social and economic transformations wrought by flexible, globalized capitalism; and finally, what kind of ethical subject emerges when the master narratives that previously regulated our language games can no longer do so.

Up until season five, Walter White is not a "man with a plan." Rather, he appears to lurch from event to event, rarely seeming to have anticipated what was coming next, almost always having to come up with an improvisatory move in which to handle a situation, only to find that the "success" of his move in the game has led to an even more difficult and unanticipated event, which now must be dealt with in its course. In episode 101, when Emilio—accompanying Krazy-8 to a meeting at the Winnebago to discuss distribution—recognizes Walt from the DEA bust that landed Emilio in jail, thus making it likely that Walt and Jesse will not get out of the desert alive, Walt improvises an instructional cook for the two men in which he concocts a poisonous gas instead of the expected meth and locks the two of them in the Winnebago to suffocate to death. But as we know, Krazy-8 doesn't die, so Walt is confronted with yet another situation in which he must improvise a way out.

This happens over and over again in the series, in too many instances to enumerate: we can take as emblematic the scene in episode 508 ("Gliding over All") when Skyler takes Walt to the shabby corrugated

4.1. Eradication of the ethnic enclave

metal storage unit to show him the tens of millions of dollars in cash his activities have yielded, way beyond anything the car wash business could possibly launder. The money here, far from being the accumulated wealth of any calculated business plan, is more or less useless, except as the marker of Walt's successive moves in the game, like the score on a pinball machine.

Walt's general modus operandi is thus the opposite of that of Gus Fring, who meticulously plots out every move in his business. Gus's carefully planned elimination of the Eladio Mexican cartel (410, "Salud"; fig. 4.1), for example, requires that Gus build up Jesse's confidence over several weeks (and introduce a distance in Jesse's relationship to Walt); that Jesse will be able to rise to the occasion when cooking for the cartel once in Mexico (which he does, to Mike's proud surprise); that all the members of the gang will partake in the toast with the rare tequila Gus has poisoned; that he will be able to take a perfectly timed bathroom break, during which he will be able to vomit up his stomach contents, knowing that the cartel will have made him take the first drink from the gift bottle; and, as a final precaution, that Mike and Jesse will be able to rush him to a state-of-the-art medical facility he has thrown together inside a tent nearby, so that any lingering effects of the poison can be treated.

Gus, that is, controls the narrative of his empire with minute precision, in contrast to Walt. Indeed, before they agree to do business together, Gus has qualms about Walt's reliability, and while this is ostensibly because of his association with Jesse—a "user"—we sense that he's also criticizing Walter's sentimental attachments, which could bring instability to the business. In any case, in his early dealings with Walt, it seems clear that he has Walt pegged as a reliable "clock puncher" and not much more. (Note how Walt meticulously prepares his lunch sandwiches for his first day on the new job—carefully trimming off the "nonwhite" crust of the generic white bread—and then writes his name on the paper bag, as if he were headed to an auto plant!) Gus doesn't yet see Walt's nascent adeptness in playing language games.

Gus's calculation is evident even at the start of his business career, when, in a flashback in episode 408 ("Hermanos"), he and his partner/lover Max present the head of the Mexican cartel the proposition that switching from cocaine to crystal meth would eliminate the cartel's reliance on Colombia for product and thus increase profits exponentially. It's in this flashback that we see the horrifying and arbitrary murder of Max, shot in the head from behind by Tio Salamanca, presumably at the orders of the don, who felt that the initiative shown by the two men was somehow an affront to his authority. This brutal murder—which Gus will spend a lifetime trying to avenge, even if the avenging is fully integrated into his calculated scheme to advance his business empire—can be characterized as an act of radical evil: it is evil that is fully willed, as if the moral order is being destroyed "from within." Interestingly, Gus performs a similar act in episode 401 ("Box Cutter"), when he slits the throat of his guard Victor simply to deliver a message to the horrified Walt and Jesse looking on. (To be sure, Victor messed up in his assignment to stop Jesse from killing Gale: he allowed onlookers to see him and potentially be able to identify him. But it only compounds the horror when Gus uses this mistake as an occasion to stage a murder for show.) These murders of Max, Victor, and later Andrea at the hands of the neo-Nazi gang form a series that pushes us toward an unfathomable horror and darkness at the heart of human life.

It isn't until the end of season four that Walt—knowing that his days are numbered and that Gus plans to "replace" (as in, kill) him—begins to actively take control of the narrative "game." But even here, he must constantly improvise and shift gears. For example, in episode 412 ("End Times"), Gus inexplicably senses that a bomb has been planted in his car and walks away with his guards, while Walt, on a rooftop nearby, watches in frustration. It's as if Gus's command of the narrative extends so far that he can even read Walt's mind, thus forcing Walt to improvise a plan that will so play on Gus's blind spot that Gus will fail to see it. The result is the famous climax of episode 413 ("Face Off"), in which Walter has recruited the enfeebled Tio to turn himself into a suicide bomb—Tio feeling he has nothing to live for since Gus eradicated the last male bearer of the Salamanca family name in the massacre in episode 410—with the bomb cleverly rigged to the little bell he uses to communicate. But even before these attempts to kill Gus, Walter needed first to break the bond that Gus had cleverly made with Jesse, so that Walt could pull Jesse into his plan.

This is where the lily of the valley plot comes in. Presumably (we are never given anything more than suggestive hints until Walt confesses his act at the very end of the series) he has given Brock, the young son of Andrea, a carefully titrated dose of the poisonous blossoms of lily of the valley so that he can then convince Jesse that Gus was the one behind the poisoning. Yet even this idea is born, at the beginning of 412, as the beleaguered and seemingly defeated Walt sits at a table playing spin the bottle with his .38 revolver, which ends up pointing to him twice before it points to the lily of the valley plant. Are we to read this as signifying that his life is over until he is suddenly struck with an idea about the plant? Or that the lily of the valley plot effectively destroys him as a human being? Certainly, the poisoning of the innocent boy is morally despicable, partaking of that radical evil I noted earlier, and perhaps this is why the series hides the act, showing us only shots of the plant in Walt's patio while leaving obscure how Walt managed to get the boy to ingest it. But I would suggest that here, Walt's crime is fundamentally different from that horrific series of murders noted earlier, in that Walt is fully confident that he can calculate the precise amount of the poison to use so that the boy will not die. Once again, Walt is absolutely committed to the idea of a completely rational universe, where cause and effect coincide with no leftover or remainder, just as he was as a young

4.2. Eradication of the floating pool of "marginals"

graduate student in episode 103, breaking down the chemical composition of the human body (discussed in chapter 1).

Things take a different turn, however, in episode 508, when Walt uses the prison contacts of the neo-Nazi gang to arrange for the systematic killings of all the incarcerated former associates of Gus, men whom Mike had been paying off to keep silent (considering it a "legacy cost" of doing business), but who Walt perceives as a continual threat to him so long as they are alive (fig. 4.2). These murders are presented as a montage, set to the incongruously upbeat tune "Pick Yourself Up" sung by Nat King Cole, in which the gruesome prison murders are punctuated with a few shots of a solitary Walter studying his watch. To understand the import of this strange scene, we can begin by noting that the montage has deep resonances with what is likely the archetypal murder montage in the American cultural imaginary: Michael Corleone's elimination of all his enemies while serving as godfather to his infant nephew in *The Godfather*, afterward saying to the infant's father (the traitorous brother-in-law whose murder will shortly thereafter be the cherry on the top of this spree of violence) that he's resolved all the family business in one fell swoop.

But in the first part of *The Godfather*, the ethnic enclave still has viability, can still provide the horizon of interpretation for the events in the story (i.e., internecine wars for dynastic succession); it hasn't yet been supplanted by the privatized and assimilated middle-class family that became a central focus of television in the 1950s. (See the semiotic square, fig. I.11, in the introduction.) Throughout *Breaking Bad*, Gus has been engaged in systematically wiping out the ethnic enclave, but we get no sense that he has been deeply connected to anyone after the cartel has killed his partner Max. Strictly speaking, he's a figure of "no future"—a pure death drive—which is exactly why the series must present its homosexual characters as governed by what today might seem like the outmoded logic of "the open secret." As Lee Edelman and others have pointed out, the subversiveness (and the allure) of homosexuality, that which forces it to hide in plain sight—and there are still those who find it subversive, despite recent gains in civil rights—lies in its refusal of the logic of reproduction, so that the future is no longer guaranteed as "the return of the same," but is rather an open potential.[7]

If we take Gus's eradication of the ethnic enclave (and the patriarchal succession that it includes) as allegorical of the latest modernization of capitalism, then Walt's arranged prison massacre can be viewed as figuring the gradual disappearance of a floating labor pool of criminals: as if in the hypervisibility of the society of the spectacle, where every surface is illuminated by the soft glow of the corporate office, the underworld itself is no longer a world underneath our own, but is, strictly speaking, continuous with it. This is how we are to understand the corporate headquarters of the transnational Madrigal corporation (introduced in the teaser to 502 ["Madrigal"]), where the even glow of fluorescent light bathing the rooms suggests that the criminal world has become fully integrated into global capitalism (fig. 4.3). In any case, it is unthinkable that the televisual family could be the locus of the kind of capital accumulation marked by Walt's barrels of unlaundered cash, and even Elliott and Gretchen Schwartz—the former business partners of Walter in the company Gray Matter, who became fabulously rich after Walter left the company (significantly, in the context of this discussion, they are childless)—seem merely the public faces of the *real* site of capital accumulation: "Gray Matter" itself. (When, in the final episode, Walt dumps his remaining cash onto a coffee table in the Schwartzes' house, the money

4.3. The Madrigal Corp: Crime is fully integrated into global capitalism

seems like a pile of dirt littering the impeccably smooth interior design of the house.)

I began this chapter by discussing the supplanting of master narratives by language games, by suggesting that the series presents us with an opposition between improvisational play and methodical planning. Now we can begin to see where this is leading us: if the financialization of capitalism renders capital more and more an abstraction, if capital has been relocated to the intangible neural flows within "gray matter," this development is strictly correlated to flexible specialization, just-in-time production processes, and a reorganization of the social around niches and micronarratives. As social scientists like Zygmunt Bauman have argued, at the level of everyday life (whether workplace, home, school, or mall), this organization demands not conformity to given rules, but rather flexibility: in Bauman's words, "a readiness to change tactics and style at short notice, to abandon commitments and loyalties without regret—and to pursue opportunities according to their current availability, rather than following one's own established preferences."[8] In this universe, to repurpose Marx's famous dictum, all that is solid—from the dynastic clan to the hermetically sealed nuclear family of television's first golden age—melts in the air.

4.4. Walt's headlong rush into the clothing store

One of the many achievements of Bryan Cranston's enactment of the character of Walter White is the way he puts into Walt's very bodily movements this quality of lurching from event to event. What's most notable about Walt's movements is that they don't seem to be fluidly responding to the affective fields around him: they always have to be channeled through his brain, which makes them seem somehow forced or unnatural. Initially, this might erroneously be ascribed to his timidity: when, at his birthday party in episode 101, Hank suddenly puts a revolver in his hands, he's completely paralyzed. In other words, his body and mind do not engage in the kind of mimetic play that would allow him to assimilate the power of the gun (the way, for example, a child might draw on its memory bank of images in order to forge relationships to newly discovered objects in the environment). But even when Walt begins to assume a more aggressive masculinity (later in the same episode!), his movements seem unnatural. When some teenage boys at a local clothing store are making fun of Walt Jr.'s disability, Walt doesn't go directly to them, but rather steals out the back door in order to burst dramatically through the front door to confront the boys. As he pushes open the door and moves toward the boys, his head leads his entire body, as if he is literally rushing "headlong" into the ensuing fray (fig. 4.4).

This kind of over-thought bodily movement makes Walt something of a "drama queen." In episode 106 ("Crazy Handful of Nothin'"), after Tuco refuses to pay Jesse for a batch of meth and then puts Jesse in the hospital with a brutal beating, Walt enters Tuco's heavily guarded lair to recover the money, armed with a large crystal that appears to be meth but is actually the highly explosive "fulminated mercury" Walt has earlier lectured about in his chemistry class. When Tuco becomes belligerent, Walt calmly picks up the crystal, announces that it is not meth, and then hurls it to the floor, where it blows out all the windows and some of the wall. Here, we can see just how the dialectic between body and will plays out: in the close-ups of Walter, we see a steely determination and an agility in playing the language game as an equal. But as he hurls the crystal, or later as he raises his arms in the face of drawn guns, his bodily movements are far from athletic and always seem to have a mental supplement, as if he feels he must force his body to express what he is thinking or feeling. Thus, his mind becomes his great asset in the games that will follow season one. Once again, though, it's less the methodically planned calculations of Gus Fring than a just-in-time calculus perfectly in keeping with the flexibility of the contemporary subject that Bauman has described so well. Ultimately, Cranston's performance gives us a body that is in some deep way not "at home in the world"—sometimes he seems to be fighting the very air around him—even as his formidable powers of mental improvisation are then channeled into his gestures in overly dramatic ways.

While I have connected this flexible, improvisational logic of events to contemporary developments in neoliberal capitalism, its aesthetic expression resonates with developments in cinematic genres of the 1960s, particularly in the spaghetti western and in the James Bond franchise (thus suggesting that nascent forms of contemporary experience were emerging in that crucial decade). Both of these genres had a global reach and appeal, and both construct narratives around the (scripted) improvisational skills of the players. The Bond films are generally taken to be aesthetically inferior to the westerns of Sergio Leone, insofar as the former deploy a rather mainstream filmic language so as to validate the Anglo-American imperium by policing the racial, ethnic, and gendered "threats" to its existence; while the latter adopt a critical stance toward the American project that was celebrated in the westerns of classical Hollywood. But both genres revel in placing their characters in dangerous, high-stakes games, where outsmarting one's opponent via a quick-witted move becomes essential for survival. Bond, of course, is assisted in his improvisation by a panoply of technological gizmos that are presented to us in a scene at the home office. This too marks the franchise as fundamentally conservative, insofar as the technophilia is always under the mastery of a representative of the technocratic elite of the mother country, thus forging a link between technology and "homeland security."

Breaking Bad, as we've seen, displays a very different kind of technophilia, one connected not to the national project but to a do-it-yourself culture that comes from below. From removing the filings from Etch A Sketch toys in order to build a device that will cut through a security lock (107, "A No-Rough-Stuff-Type Deal"), all the way up to using a giant magnet to erase Gus Fring's hard drive (501, "Live Free or Die"), the inventiveness in *Breaking Bad* refashions the ready-to-hand materials all around us. This is why the inventive play of the spaghetti western is much more closely aligned to the spirit of *Breaking Bad* than is that of the Bond franchise. The spaghetti western plays out on a terrain in which the Law has been suspended, throwing all the characters into a state of generalized warfare in which their skills at gamesmanship and improvisation become their prime assets. In short, it adopts an ethos of "street culture," which goes a long way toward explaining why the genre held such appeal for what we might call an "international subaltern" class.

Probably the most direct channeling of Leone into *Breaking Bad* occurs in episode 502, when Lydia sets up a trap for Mike Ehrmantraut to be killed by luring him to a modest bungalow. Realizing he's walking into a trap, Mike hangs a children's toy at the front door of the house, so that while the hit man's attention is directed toward the noises made by the toy at the front door, Mike sneaks in through the back door and foils the plot. This scene seems to be reprising a scene in *Once upon a Time in the West* (1968), when Cheyenne (Jason Robards), having climbed on top of the moving train where the gang is holding Harmonica (Charles Bronson) captive, uses the sound of his footsteps to lure one of the gunmen to a window outside which his cowboy boot is dangling. The gunman naturally thinks he's seeing Cheyenne's leg, until suddenly a bullet explodes from the toe of the shoe, killing the gunman, as we realize Cheyenne has outsmarted his opponents in the game.

But there is another, deeper aesthetic connection between *Breaking Bad* and the spaghetti western. This genre has a profound sense of rhythm: it presents us with a world moving at varying speeds, so that the speed of the coal-powered locomotive contrasts with the relative slowness of the outpost, or of the desert landscape itself. The human drama plays itself out against this world moving at varying speeds, and succeeding at the improvisational games requires one to have an exquisite attunement to the varying rhythms that lay out the virtual potentials surrounding the player. *Breaking Bad* takes up this play with rhythm and timing within the form of serial television—which must adapt itself to the regular interruptions of the commercial break, whether for the initial run or for syndication—thus opening up new expressive possibilities in the form. We've seen in chapter 2 how the beat structure (in its industry definition) in *Breaking Bad* pushes far beyond the norms even of the contemporary quality series. But within these longer beats are varying superimposed rhythms, ranging from the near instantaneity of the chemical reaction to the glacial slowness of the desert rocks. Between these two extremes, we can sense the comforting rhythms produced by the home (see chapter 2), the rhythms of technological devices, the rhythms of repetitions produced by compulsions (drug users, Marie's kleptomania), and so on. Embedded within all of these rhythmic forces are the most undeterminable of rhythms, those that mark the birth of human thought, that allow us to find a place for human agency within the field of potentials that surround the characters.

This concern with relative speeds underwrites one of the series' signature devices, the time-lapse photography of the urban or desert landscape. But it also can be seen in offhand details, like the hobbies taken up by Hank. In the first half of the series, his hobby is the more "volatile" microbrewing of beer, and in the period when he's in the throes of anxiety over his pending promotion to El Paso and the front line of the drug wars, he one night mistakes the popping of the caps off the beer

4.5. The abyss of the balance sheet

bottles as gunfire coming from the garage. But after he is crippled and immobile, he begins collecting "rocks" (as Marie insists on calling the minerals), immersing himself in the study of geological time.

When Walter is agonizing over whether or not he must kill Krazy-8 (103), he decides to divide a sheet of paper (on a legal pad!) into two columns in which he can list reasons for letting Krazy-8 live and for killing him. On the "Let Him Live" side, Walter comes up with bullet points like "It's the moral thing to do," "Judeo/Christian principles," "You are *not* a murderer," "Sanctity of life," "Post-traumatic stress"; when we move to the "Kill Him" side, we see just one charged bullet point: "He'll kill your entire family if you let him go" (fig. 4.5). This scene embodies the black humor that characterizes the series and mocks the simple-mindedness of the self-help and advice culture that finds such a congenial home on the internet today. But who hasn't, at one point or another when faced with a difficult decision, resorted to just such an attempt to come up with just such a balance sheet? Still, if my own experience is in any way generalizable, what we eventually realize is that either column could potentially extend to infinity, and that there is in any case no way to assign weight to a series of thoughts that are at the same time interrelated and yet fundamentally incommensurable. (Will the "post-traumatic stress" of committing a premeditated murder be the result of Walt's "Judeo-Christian principles"?) The lists quickly become an abyss of rational thoughts, received wisdom, clichés, desires, and fantasies, and when we eventually make a decision, it is less a result of the rational choice that grounds the subject of classical economic theory than it is a mysterious act of will.

Such was the view of the drives developed by the great late nineteenth-century philosopher Friedrich Nietzsche. For Nietzsche, drives were fundamentally a multiplicity: they thus disturb the binary logic of either/or that is a fundamental ideological operation underlying how modern thought has theorized human activity across the social, economic, and psychic realms. Even Freud, who was definitely influenced by the work of Nietzsche, finds the need to assign the drives to two opposing camps: life versus death, conscious versus unconscious, and so on. Deleuze, who was even more strongly influenced by Nietzsche, took Freud to task for just this reason: Freud's dualistic subject of modernity (the model for the subject that we see in expressionism and film noir) needs to be replaced with a view of the subject as multiplicity: the "I contain multitudes" of Walt Whitman. Given this view of the subject as a cacophony of disparate drives, one might wonder how anyone comes to a decision about anything. Nietzsche's answer was the will-to-power. In a sense, Walt's list gives us a humorous allegory of the process: the one item in the right column, the fantasy of his family being murdered, trumps everything in the left column. But caution is required lest we end up turning Nietzsche's will-to-power into some vulgar, Darwinian notion of survival of the fittest, which was far from what Nietzsche intended. The will-to-power for him simply marks that mysterious point in which, amid a swirl of virtual affects, something, a decision, gets actualized in the world.

A number of social theorists, taking their cues from Michel Foucault and Deleuze, have recently attempted to rethink the model of the economic subject of contemporary consumer economies along the same lines. Neoliberal economic theory takes its model for the subject to be the "rational agent" whose lineage is the entire tradition of classical economics since Adam Smith, whose "invisible hand" becomes simply the totalization of all of the rational acts of the freely acting agents. Let's bracket out for the moment the question of whether the typical subject in neoliberal economies—whose lives are made increasingly precarious by a programmatic siphoning of wealth to the rich—can be thought of as "acting freely." At a more abstract level, at least since Nietzsche and Freud, this notion of a freely acting rational subject has come to seem dubious at best, and this before the great expansion of consumerism and the penetration of the spectacle into every facet of daily life, both of which call into question the extent to which any choice—whether of toothpaste, a wardrobe, or a career—is rationally motivated. In fact, the more we look for the rationally motivated subject of classical and neoliberal economics, the more likely we are to find instead an abyss of heterogeneous drives (or, in more current parlance, affects). Brian Massumi notes how, since 2000, the literature on nonconscious decision making has gained traction among social theorists; he cites a study from 2006 which shows that the more conscious deliberation is put into a major consumer choice, paradoxically the less satisfaction that choice is likely to produce.[9] Massumi writes, in a passage that seems directly to address Walt's list-making activity: "The more calculation and rational deliberation goes into making a consumer choice such as buying a new car, the less likely the choice will be to correspond to an expert cost-to-benefit analysis, and the less satisfying the experience will be perceived to have been 'postchoice'—even independently of the issue of cost-effectiveness. Influential studies have found *a negative correlation between rational calculation and consumer satisfaction*. Nonconscious choice—intuitive 'deliberation-without-attention'—produced 'better' choices."[10]

To pull the various strands of the arguments in this chapter together, I'll begin by noting that the great war between Gus Fring and Walter White presents two very different models of subjectivity. Gus is the old dualistic subject who freely chooses evil. Walt—though his moral choices are often, to be sure, abominable—is a subject who is buffeted hither and thither as he improvises his way through a succession of language games. Out of this, an ethical conundrum emerges: if we are to have an ethics of pure immanence, one that valorizes the creative engagement with the world as it presents itself to us, then what are we to say of the reprehensible results of Walter White's adventure? To begin to answer this, we need to understand that in *Breaking Bad*, the (scripted) improvisation and game play take on a double valence. On the one hand, they are strictly speaking a *symptom*: they index a mode of being specific to contemporary neoliberal culture, in which, in the face of increasing downward mobility, when one cannot reasonably expect to be able to afford hot water to bathe in, let alone an insurance plan that will prevent you from going bankrupt when faced with major illness or accident, the only stance to take is one of flexibility, improvisation, and preemptiveness in the face of an increasingly precarious future. On the other hand, however, they come to figure a kind of aesthetic ideal (to which I will return in chapter 5), a potentially—but *only* potentially—liberatory way to engage with the world.

Foucault famously saw Deleuze and Guattari's embrace of a pure creativity as providing us with a handbook for "the non-fascist life."[11] Fascism here is to be taken as a power that forces creative energies into repressive and exhausted forms, like "the homeland," and given Foucault's networked understanding of power, he finds that fascism works by reproducing its structures within institutions like the school, the factory, and the family. In this way, Walter White's "inadequate ideas" channel his creativity into "his own private fascism," which as we've seen is expressively enacted in a body that is fiercely under the rule of his mind. Think here of the many ways Walt enacts this through the series; a seemingly minor incident can be paradigmatic. When Walt Jr. is learning to drive (204, "Down"), given the limitations of movement in his lower body, he quite naturally and comfortably uses one foot to operate the gas pedal and the other to operate the brake. This is a creative and active engagement with the event of Walt-Jr.-driving-a-car. But Walter—obsessed with a preconceived (and in this case inadequate) idea of the "proper" way to drive, no doubt only a corollary of larger ideas about what it means to "be a man"—insists that Walt Jr. use one foot to operate both, with predictably disastrous results. This is an example of fascism reproducing itself at the micro level of the family.

I'll conclude with the following. We've seen how "Gray Matter"—and I take the company name here to be emblematic of the larger movement toward an economy centered on immaterial labor and the production and management of flows of attention and affect—is the site par excellence of neoliberal capital accumulation. But the gray in Gray Matter, we learn early on, is the result of a kind of Hegelian synthesis between the surnames of Elliott Schwartz (black, in German) and Walter White. Contrast this gray to the blue in Walt's crystal meth. This blue is strictly speaking a "nothing"; the scientists who have commented on the show's chemistry tell us that there is nothing in Walt's formula for cooking that would produce a blue tint in his product.[12] Thus, the blue is precisely that surplus, that excess, that is the one notion Walt cannot understand or accept. We could, following Lacan, call this blue the "object *a*," the acceptance of and fidelity to which marks the end of a successful psychoanalysis. But we needn't bring Lacan in here to understand that if only Walter White could have understood this "nothing" at the center of his creative energies, it might have allowed him finally to feel at home in the world, might have given his body "grace."

5 Immanence: A Life

The violent battle between the neo-Nazi gang and Hank and Steve Gomez of the DEA—with an arrested and handcuffed Walt stuck helplessly in the middle, and Jesse hidden in a ditch under the car—spans episodes 513 ("To'hajiilee") and 514 ("Ozymandias"), with 513 being truly a cliffhanger. This battle becomes actualized by way of a series of maneuvers that is perhaps the series' most finely calibrated interplay among game play, improvisation, and timing (both bad and good)—a fundamental aesthetic mode in the series. Here, Jesse is at last able to outsmart Walter in an elaborate game that will lure him to the desert hiding spot of his drug money.

The DEA has already learned from informants that Walter used a rental van to drive his barrels of cash somewhere off-road in the desert; this information is the result of a clever game in which Jesse, now cooperating with the DEA, poses for a fake cell phone photo showing him lying next to a pile of bloody cow brains in order to make the informant Huell think Walter has killed Jesse and is now after Huell. Although it turns out the rental agency does not keep GPS records of its rented vehicles, Hank realizes that Walter will not know that, and thus that Jesse can lure him to the incriminating site simply by telling him he has tracked down the money using the rental van's GPS and is there waiting, burning the money in thousand-dollar increments until Walter arrives. Naturally, Walt speeds to the burial site, which allows the DEA to track his movements. When he finds the site deserted, it dawns on him that he must have been set up, though he doesn't yet know what the next move in the game is going to be. Realizing he must improvise a way out of the trap, Walt phones the neo-Nazi gang and gives them the GPS coordinates of the burial site.

When Jesse, Hank, and Steve Gomez arrive on the scene, a shocked and defeated Walter surrenders, seemingly having forgotten that he has invited the neo-Nazi gang to the game. The gang arrives after Walt has been handcuffed, read his Miranda rights, and placed under arrest in the back seat of the DEA car (and after Hank has telephoned Marie with the news that Walt has at long last been captured). And here—with all guns drawn and the two camps facing each other in a standoff—we get a particularly strong evocation of the characteristic tempo of the spaghetti western, as all the parties are calculating the strengths of their respective hands and weighing what card to play next. Against the glacial slowness of the desert terrain, action is temporarily suspended while thought accelerates to lightning speed, and everything resolves to a question of timing. But finally, the leader of the gang must realize that the cards have been dealt in his favor: the gang begins firing, Hank and Gomez fire back, and suddenly, amid the flurry of automatic weapons firing back and forth, the episode ends.

The playing out of the gun battle continues in episode 514, but only after one of the more resonant teasers of the series, a scene that unfolds in the exact same location as the gun battle, but some two years earlier, when Walt and Jesse have chosen the site as the perfect spot to begin cooking in the Winnebago. Here, the natural light has an enveloping, golden diffuseness, as opposed to the ferocity with which it beats down on the desert most often in season five. We see the easy familiarity from which Walter and Jesse will develop their surrogate father-son relationship (particularly wrenching now that we know Walt has put a hit order on Jesse). And we see the first lie to Skyler, the first in a series that will decimate the marriage from within, ultimately transforming it into just another "mom and pop" business operation. Interestingly, before his phone call, we see Walter rehearsing out loud the story he's going to tell Skyler; he hasn't yet discovered his hidden talent for spur-of-the-moment improvisation. But at this point, Skyler still trusts Walt implicitly; and only the block of knives sitting unused on the counter next to Skyler introduces an instability to the conversation (fig. 5.1): two years later (and two episodes earlier in the series), Skyler will have

5.1. The block of knives will become Skyler's weapon two years later

pulled out one of those knives to use as a weapon against Walt, cutting his hand before they writhe on the floor as Walt attempts to take the knife, and Walt Jr. finally manages to pull his father away. (Even here, there is humor: Walter then stands up and screams, "What the hell is wrong with you? We're a *family*!")

What is most interesting aesthetically about this teaser is the way it ends. Walt stands alone in the desert landscape, with the Winnebago behind him in the distance, and he fades out of the image (fig. 5.2). After that, the Winnebago fades from the image, and we are left with only the quiet desert landscape, whose quiet we know will soon be interrupted by the gunfire that ended the previous episode. Two things are remarkable about this shot. First is the way it suggests that the landscape of the desert has preserved traces of events of the past: this flashback is not assigned to the mind of any of the characters in the scene, but presents us rather with a profoundly impersonal memory, a "world memory," if you will. This leads directly to the second remarkable aspect of the shot: as the image of Walt fades away and is absorbed into the desert landscape, we begin to feel that we have been bearing witness to a life, a life that is utterly singular and is now careening toward its end.

What does it mean when televisual seriality—instead of being an indefinitely extended series destined to end only from irrelevance or old

5.2. Walt disappears into the landscape

age—has a determined end point? It would seem that the indefinitely extended series aligns conceptually (though not of course formally) with televisual "liveness" and temporal synchronization, whereas the series that from the get-go is forging its unique "path to death" offers us different durations to inhabit.[1] There are two ways in which televisual seriality can give us "a life." The first—most typical of serial television—gives us life as a kind of ongoing sociality that is contiguous with and parallels the family circle (however loosely defined), which is its audience: we live our lives alongside the everyday adventures, as well as the more singular rites of passage and decisive life events, of Lucy and Ricky, Richard Kimble, Archie and Edith, Tony Soprano and the gang. *Breaking Bad* gives us this more common sense of life lived as well. But the cinematic devices that bridge episodes 513 and 514 bring a different, more radical sense to the notion of "a life": just as there is an impersonal world memory, so too is there a life that logically precedes any particular life of any particular individual with a name. Walt may be possessed by the idea that became a branding device for the series ("Remember My Name"), but at the very end, there is a man, hovering between life and death, blood leaving his body from a massive wound; a man whose bloody hand leaves a mark on the stainless steel tank as he falls to the

5.3. Walt leaves his mark

ground (fig. 5.3).[2] And amid all the horror, this life produces in us a kind of strange wonder.

This is all despite the fact that everything is in ruins at the end of *Breaking Bad*. Has any other television series dared to lead us to such a point of utter darkness, with seemingly no exit? Dared to undermine so thoroughly those very ideals that television has tended so vigilantly to protect? Home: the White house is now boarded up, vandalized, a mirror of the crack houses that Walt's drugs produced as a social by-product. Family: Skyler and Walt Jr. are now living in a shabby apartment where the knotty pine woodwork competes for attention with the putrid-colored linoleum covering the kitchen floor. And the Law? Its two major representatives in the series are now decomposing in a grave site somewhere in the desert, the GPS coordinates of which are the numbers on an expired Lotto ticket, which Walt gives Skyler at their last meeting so that she might use the information to cut a deal with the federal prosecutors doing all they can to make her life as impoverished as possible. (Talk about hitting the jackpot!) Ironically, once the case moves into the machinery of the juridical arm of government, we see more clearly than ever how everyday life under neoliberalism manifests itself as generalized warfare.

5.4. Walt's spectral image

In this scene, Walter's last meeting with Skyler (516, "Felina"), Walt is once again presented as spectral, as one of the living dead. There is, to begin with, the often-discussed shot in Skyler's new apartment, in which the camera gazes from a distance at Skyler at the kitchen table, the screen bisected by the large wooden pillar of an archway, as on the phone Marie is warning Skyler that Walt has returned and is on the loose in Albuquerque. When the phone conversation ends, the camera dollies left to reveal that Walt has been in the kitchen the entire time, hidden behind the pillar by the camera positioning but now "unveiled" by the camera move. After he leaves, he hangs around to get a last glimpse of the son who now loathes him, lurking behind corners so as not to be spotted, until finally, photographed through the glass of a window, his image begins to blur into the background as he walks away (fig. 5.4).

At this point, I need to specify more clearly what I mean by "*a* life," with the indefinite article. The title of this chapter is taken directly from one of Gilles Deleuze's last essays, dense and allusive, and written when he was wracked with illness and in the year he took his own life. In "Immanence: A Life," Deleuze is attempting to come up with a purely immanent conception of life. Immanence requires that a life be thought before, and outside of, any consideration of a self or an object world, for these latter—individuals, objects—already enmesh us in determinations, causes and effects, character, and so on. But for Deleuze, the critical issue for philosophy is to preserve a space from which the new can emerge, an open space of potentials, an Outside, "beyond good and evil." Deleuze uses a character from Charles Dickens's *Our Mutual Friend* as an example: as an individual, the dying man was a pathetic scoundrel hated by everyone, but as he lies in a coma and near death, everyone around him becomes mesmerized with wonder at every little sign of life the body exhibits. The better he gets, the more the wonder falls back into hatred or contempt, as he begins to move away from the virtuality of "*a* life" and back to the individual that he was in "*his* life." But the indefinite article is critical: Deleuze here is not referring to some sort of vitalist "life force"—for that would simply be to subordinate the event to yet another transcendental concept. Rather, he is referring to the idea that there is "a" life that is logically prior to the particular descriptions that any given life takes on.[3] "A life" points to the Outside, to an open, virtual field from which any individual life becomes actualized and in which any individual life is a "vantage point."[4] It is all the virtual potentials that surround a person, before any act materializes, that give us a concept of life that is strictly immanent to life: "immanence: a life."

Perhaps the greatest cinematic presentation of "a life" occurs at the end of Martin Scorsese's *Taxi Driver* (1976). Following his murder spree, Travis Bickle (Robert De Niro), his face drenched in blood, sits on the sofa inside the shabby apartment where Iris (Jody Foster) turns tricks, and as the police enter the scene with guns drawn, Travis just lifts his finger to his bloody head and mimics blowing his own brains out. At this point, as we stare in horrified wonder at the events that have just actualized before our eyes, we see Travis as "a life." Travis Bickle will return to *his* life, now as a banal folk hero—until, that is, those final moments in the film, when something indeterminate flashes in the mirror, his eyes dart, his head jerks, something new is happening . . . Now certainly, one could argue that Travis Bickle is locked into a repetition compulsion, is a pure death drive, and one could cite all of the film's circular camera movements to argue that this final shot suggests the cycle is about to begin again. But from the point of view of "a life," that little chain of micro-events at the end of the film is, strictly speaking, something new, something coming from the Outside, something with unpredictable effects.

The final episode of *Breaking Bad* is haunted by *Taxi Driver*. In the teaser of the episode, when Walter White—who at the end of the previous episode has essentially turned himself in by telephoning the police in the bar, but then changes course upon seeing Elliott and Gretchen being interviewed by Charlie Rose—sits in a car whose snow- and ice-covered windows hide him from the police racing to the scene, the blue and red police lights smear across the windows in much the way that the Manhattan landscape becomes a phantasmagoria reflected in Travis Bickle's windshield (figs. 5.5 and 5.6). Even the close-ups of the eyes and the shots of the rearview mirror take us back to that film. Then there is Walt's careful assembling of the homemade weapon triggered by the trunk-door remote, which reprises Travis Bickle's more modest sliding revolver track. Yet another echo comes when Lydia puts the poisoned Stevia into her cup and the overhead camera moves into an extreme close-up of the tea; this recalls the shot in *Taxi Driver*—a shot that first appears in relation to a coffee cup, in Jean-Luc Godard's 1967 film *Two or Three Things I Know about Her*—where the camera moves into the bubbling Alka-Seltzer in Travis's water glass.

But it is *Breaking Bad*'s final aerial shot that restages the shot in *Taxi Driver* of "a life." In *Taxi Driver*, after Travis's suicidal gesture, we cut to the camera looking directly down at the scene (turning the room into a kind of architectural elevation); the camera begins a tracking shot that ends up turning this view into a kind of moving tableau, taking in the bloody bodies, the shell-shocked Iris, and finally the two uniformed cops, frozen as they stand in the doorway with guns pointed at Travis (fig. 5.7).[5] In *Breaking Bad*, after Walt falls to the ground, the camera, looking directly down on his body, begins an aerial ascent that, as in *Taxi Driver*, gives us a schematic, architectural view of the space, as we then see the police move in with guns drawn (fig. 5.8). This is the final shot of the series.

In *Taxi Driver*, the overhead tracking shot is followed by a series of moving camera shots, connected by dissolves, which retrace in reverse Travis's murderous itinerary, back through the narrow staircase and landing, out through the lobby, and finally into the street, now crowded

5.5. *Taxi Driver* (Martin Scorsese, 1976): The urban phantasmagoria

5.6. Echoes of *Taxi Driver* in the final episode

5.7. *Taxi Driver*: Overhead shot of police

5.8. Final shot of the series

with onlookers. In the world of *Taxi Driver*, the actions that have taken place can still be situated within a public sphere, where they will circulate and take on meaning. New York City in the mid-1970s was on the verge of bankruptcy, to the point where the city was seen as ungovernable, as having slid into a kind of Hobbesian state of nature. From our vantage point today, we can see this as simply an early moment in the "creative destruction" that has refashioned our cities according to the logic of neoliberalism. This is a logic that cedes more and more public space to privatization, the prime example being the "cleaning up"—or, from another angle, the "Disneyfication"—of Times Square in the 1990s era of Mayor Rudy Giuliani. As writers like Samuel Delaney have shown, what the spaces of the old Times Square allowed for—and what is now foreclosed—was a public sphere built through an intermingling (or intercourse, both literal and figurative) that cut across all sorts of ethnic, racial, sexual, and class boundaries.[6] And while *Taxi Driver* often seems to adopt a panicked position in relation to the street—this is what makes it part of the "right cycle" elaborated in the introduction—it still manages to give us an image of a pluralist public sphere in these shots outside the tenement.[7]

By contrast, *Breaking Bad*'s final shot remains trapped in the interior of the neo-Nazi compound; the shot thus resembles the final shot of episode 411 ("Crawl Space"), in which the camera cranes up from Walter lying in the crawl space (discussed in chapter 2; fig. 2.5). In both cases, we remain locked within a privatized space—the family home, the neo-Nazi take on "the gated community"—in which our sense of the Outside has been foreclosed. Already the series has thematized this foreclosure of the Outside, in its systematic destruction of the residual cultures of the ethnic enclave, or in its suggestions that the Czech Republic, in a post-Communist frenzy of capital accumulation, has become a vast new market for drugs. This becomes the aesthetic tension that informs the final moments of the series: the sense that at the macro level, there is no more Outside to be found, while at the micro level, in the presentation of Walter as "a life," the sense that the Outside is always present, always *insists* between the spaces of our lives as individuals and histories.[8]

There is, however, an alternative way in which this last episode presents us with "a life," and that is in the figure of Jesse Pinkman. After

5.9. Jesse's line of flight

the massacre of the neo-Nazis via the remote-operated machine gun in the trunk of Walt's car, Jesse strangles the still-alive Todd as revenge for Todd's cold-blooded murders of Drew Sharp (the boy on the dirt bike during the train robbery) and Andrea. A gravely wounded Walt slides a gun to Jesse and tells him to "do it" (kill Walt), but Jesse drops the gun and says, "Do it yourself." Then Jesse gets into a car, floors the accelerator, crashes through the gate of the compound, and in a pure line of flight, speeds toward an unknown future (fig. 5.9). We see him in close-up in the speeding car. Is he laughing or crying? Is he sane or insane? All we get in these shots is pure speed and affect, as we (and Jesse) hurtle toward an absolute Outside: we are in a state of pure potentials, pure virtualities waiting to be actualized. In this sense, Jesse gives us the most profound image of "a life," in keeping with his having been the moral center of the universe of *Breaking Bad*. Jesse literally breaks the shackles of fascism, while Walter chooses to make it his final resting place.

I ended chapter 4 with the question of how an ethics based on improvisation and creative engagement with the world might lead us away from the microfascisms of the institutions of everyday life and toward what Michel Foucault called the nonfascist life. The notion of "a life" hints at

5.10. Jesse's "golden" memory

a way of more deeply understanding this question. Considering life immanently does not mean that any choice or any action is as good as any other; rather, it means believing that life is, from moment to moment, absolutely open. In the final episode, Walt's actions are fueled by ressentiment and the desire for revenge, all stemming from his inadequate ideas. Jesse, in contrast, forces Walt to confront at least one of those inadequate ideas. When Walt asks Jesse to kill him, he tries to convince Jesse by saying to him, "You know you want this," thus slyly attempting to poison Jesse with guilt. But Jesse forces Walt to say that he, Walt, is the one who wants to be shot by Jesse, whereupon Jesse tells him to do it himself. Jesse, that is, rejects ressentiment and has finally detached himself affectively from Walt. After that, Jesse throws himself into a line of flight, a pure becoming whose end point we cannot fathom; but we do sense that whatever happens, Jesse will, unlike Walt, prove himself to be worthy of the events that come to him.

The final episode gives us yet another hint at the implications of "a life"—in that remarkable "golden" moment when Jesse has a dream-memory of having made a beautiful wooden box in high school shop class (fig. 5.10). Never mind that instead of giving it to his mother, he traded it for some weed. What we see here, from within a world engulfed in darkness, is quite simply the light of creativity, of art. It is this artistic creativity that perhaps best explains how we are to understand a purely immanent ethics, improvisational rather than superegoic, the ethics of "a life." Indeed, in philosophy and critical theory since the turn of the millennium, there has been an intense new interest in the question of aesthetics, and specifically in relation to the idea that the artwork at its best destabilizes our relationship to the fixed categories through which we habitually see the world. To use Steven Shaviro's phrase, the artwork throws us into a state where we are "without criteria" to judge or even to comprehend; it thus compels us to perceive something new, and so forces us into thought.[9]

All this suggests that the practice most in keeping with the idea of the nonfascist life is the practice of art. Even in Walter White's "art," the artistry is not in the exceptional purity of the product (which is a technicist question, tied to industrial practices of measurement and standardization), but in the "blue," the unexplainable nothing that so fascinates everyone (which is an aesthetic question). Ultimately, I will argue that all of the aesthetic strategies adopted by *Breaking Bad* and explored in these pages attest to how the series affirms this artistic creativity as an ultimate value. To lead in to that discussion, it will prove useful to look at how art—in the form of poetry—circulates within the series. Here we have two cases to consider: Walt Whitman's *Leaves of Grass*, and Percy Shelley's "Ozymandias."

The circulating volume of *Leaves of Grass* in the series can be seen as a marker of an erotics of the body, and more specifically of a latent or repressed homosexual desire. (Interestingly, in *Between Men*, Eve Kosofsky Sedgwick notes how in late nineteenth-century Britain, the circulating "Whitmaniana" became "the currency of a new community that saw itself created in Whitman's image.")[10] John Champagne, in an excellent article reviewing the claims and counterclaims of Whitman scholars over whether he is to be seen as gay, argues that if Foucault is to be taken seriously—if "the homosexual," as "personnage and case history," was not invented until 1871—then we need to look at Whitman in relation to a historical epoch in which gayness such as we know it today did not exist. Whitman's celebration of comradeship (whether eroticized or not, whether given overt sexual expression or not) must then be situated within a nineteenth-century American tradition celebrating deep male friendships; it becomes, Champagne astutely notes, one of the conditions of possibility for the modern homosexual. Champagne concludes that the real danger in Whitman is in the way this celebration of a radically democratic comradeship threatens to undermine key binary oppositions that organize life and that allow for a perpetuation of oppressive hierarchies.[11] Such is the contaminated gift Gale gives to Walter. When the volume finally lands in the hands of Hank—at the moment when this least flexible, most rigid character is moving his bowels—the anxiety that overcomes him is tremendous: he feels he's just been "screwed royally" (508, "Gliding over All").

This queer or anti-Oedipal reading of Whitman can be taken farther, especially in relation to Whitman's use of anaphora, or the endless lists that link all sorts of disparate objects together in a nonhierarchical series. D. H. Lawrence commented on this in his sometimes scathing, sometimes sympathetic, often very funny essay on the poet: "All those lists of things boiled in one pudding-cloth! No, no! I don't want all those things inside me, thank you"; or, "His poems . . . are long sums in addition and multiplication, of which the answer is invariably M Y S E L F." In fact, Lawrence's essay begins in a veritable panic over the loss of boundaries, the "oozing," the "leaking," all things "merging" toward "the Mundane Egg." He does, though, farther along in the essay, praise Whitman for overturning the moralism of his literary predecessors in a new morality of "life." In his words: "It is a new great doctrine. A doctrine of life. A new great morality. A morality of actual living, not of salvation. Europe has never got beyond the morality of salvation. America to this day is deathly sick with saviourism. But Whitman, the greatest and the first and the only American teacher, was no Saviour. His morality was no morality of salvation. His was a morality of the soul living her life, not saving herself."[12]

Perhaps because of Lawrence's sympathies with Nietzsche, he is able to see in Whitman an overturning of a morality based on transcendentals in favor of an ethics that is strictly immanent to life. But he is unable to see any way for the bonding between men, or the radical democracy it might promise, to function even as an analogy for the "transvaluation of all values," to use Nietzsche's phrase. This impasse at the heart of Lawrence's thought, it seems to me, remains with us even today and manifests as a cultural symptom: in *Breaking Bad*, it manifests in the way that the series keeps pushing at the boundaries of the family while being unable to imagine anything beyond it (except the power of its own art).

The third-to-last episode, 514, takes its title from Shelley's sonnet "Ozymandias." In one sense, the story of the vain and powerful ancient king whose monument now lies in ruins is a parallel to Walter White's vanity and hubris. But on another level, the poem presents us with the implacable and terrifying power of the inorganic, of the vast desert that operates in geological time, indifferent to the travails of human action. We've already seen how, as *Breaking Bad* moves toward its conclusion, the desert landscape of New Mexico seems to take on more and more of this primal power, as the humans enact their self-destructive rituals on its stage. What's problematic in Shelley's poem is the position of the artist: Is art just another vain human enterprise destined to fall into obscurity and ruin, as did the great work of the unknown sculptor? Or can it somehow thwart the destruction wrought by "chemistry," to achieve the timeless (as, presumably, the poet hopes to have achieved in writing the poem)?

All of these ideas are thematized in the celebrated opening credits to the series. These show the periodic table, as the series title is generated from the building blocks "Br" and "Ba." This is followed by a "[Cr]eated by Vince Gilligan" card, after which the opening credits are superimposed on the opening scenes of the episode. And in every proper name, we see highlighted a letter or sequence of letters signifying an element on the periodic table. The proper name is a fundamental mark of individuation; but as I have argued, there is always "a life" that is logically prior to the proper name. As the credits suggest, there is never a name that can't be linked to the molecular power of matter in itself. Analogously, the plots and characters of the television series keep us at the level of the human; it is mise-en-scène that has the power to introduce another scale—molecular or glacial—to the images, to push us outside the representational.

Interestingly, though, in Vince Gilligan's title card, no elemental symbol is highlighted in his name; the symbol has been moved to the Cr (chromium) in "Created by." Are we thus confronted here with a sly reinstatement of the transcendental? With the idea that, of course, "the Creator" must lie outside the creation rather than be immanent to it? Perhaps. But one of the many uses of chromium is to add tint or coloration to glass; in this way, the artistic creation of the series aligns itself with the mysterious blue "nothing" that is Walter White's most enduring creation.

Chemistry is the creative power of matter itself. This creative power moves both at the lightning speed of the molecular and with the glacial slowness of the desert; somewhere in between the two, it transects the human. In his *Cinema* books, Deleuze borrowed from Henri Bergson the idea of the "center of indetermination" to indicate the way in which not just the human, but all material entities partake of the Open. This is to say that there is always a gap between cause and effect—more so in the case of humans, less so in the case of rocks, but always insuring that the next instant in time is radically open to chance, to difference, and is not reducible to the calculations of science or philosophy. Even as Walter White adopts the name Heisenberg, he nevertheless is unable to accede to or embrace this fundamental openness. And perhaps it is this very thematic strand in *Breaking Bad* that then allows the series to mobilize the cinematic so as to make *us* see this uncertainty principle operating at the heart of things. The favoring of intensive relationships of mise-en-scène over the extensive development of cause-effect chains is but one of these elements of the cinematic, though perhaps the most decisive of the many other aesthetic strategies I've talked about in the preceding pages.

At this point I must emphasize that this gap between cause and effect extends over the entire material world, which is precisely what orients the world—or "a life"—toward the Open. The improvisational experimentation of art is simply one way to allow us to see this. *Breaking Bad*'s immersion in the art of the cinematic is what allows us to see the latent forces that are arrayed between bodies in space, whether those bodies be the piled-up junk autos, the objects in the police evidence vault, or the humans arrayed across the desert landscape. For Walter Benjamin as well as for Deleuze, this was the originality and power of the cinema (or what I am calling "the cinematic"): that it could throw things into new and unexpected relations and in so doing provoke in us a new awareness or understanding. For Deleuze, the stakes were nothing less than the rekindling of a "belief in this world,"[13] something that seems all the more urgent in an epoch when more and more of our experience is consigned to the ethereal flows of spectacle.

One of the most memorable of the many musical montages of *Breaking Bad*, the one set to Tommy James and the Shondells' "Crystal Blue Persuasion" (508), presents the city as an assemblage (figs. 5.11–5.13). Linear time is suspended while all sorts of disparate objects, spaces, and people are thrown together in unlikely combinations: the cases of Coca-Cola with the insides hollowed out to hold the stacks of cash; the familiar file folder cases with the interlocking blue-flap lids to hold drugs; the shimmering, confetti-like crystals of the catalyst—all part of a vast procession of characters and vehicles moving through space, cutting into the flows of drugs and money. Is the point of all this really to show us how the drug trade operates? Or is it rather to reengage us with the wondrous energies of all the objects and spaces around us? (As the song says, "It's a new vibration.")

The montage suspends linear time in yet another way, when we consider how the song is so firmly situated within a certain historical moment in post-1968 youth culture. On YouTube there is a remarkable proto-music video that seems to have been made to accompany the hit song—perhaps a promo?—although its origins and credits are obscure.[14] In the video, the street sign at the Haight Ashbury intersection is a key shot, and the rest of the video largely juxtaposes celebratory images of youth and drug culture with more-ominous images of police and civil unrest. It's hard to imagine a more perfect set of images with which to understand where Foucault and Deleuze conceived of everyday fascism and the possibility of a nonfascist life. Thinking about the two montages together—the video and the *Breaking Bad* montage—we see flashing up before us, in a great historical short circuit, a utopian moment that the emergent discourses of neoliberalism would do everything in their power to stamp out. Yet the utopian moment survives in the thought, the philosophy, that was generated in its wake—and perhaps it is lying

5.11–5.13. “Crystal Blue Persuasion”:
The city as assemblage and flow

in wait, ready to unfurl its power in some unexpected future conjunction of possibilities.

This spectral eruption of the 1960s in the "Crystal Blue Persuasion" montage reminds us, though, of the ways in which the classical and postclassical cinema haunt *Breaking Bad*. I hope my examination of all these evocations of the cinematic archive has made clear that—and I know I am repeating myself here—they have little or nothing in common with the kind of showy citations that are a staple of postmodern filmmaking. Rather, they are an active engagement with the cinematic past. *Breaking Bad* looks to the expressive problems that confronted the filmmakers of the past and then uses their solutions to these problems as a starting point for thinking through its own expressive problems. It understands that the problem of a schoolteacher unable to afford hot water meant one thing in 1956, which then provides avenues to imagine the quite different meaning it has in 2008. We understand, though, that there is a history that has brought us here, and that rises up like a ghost to shatter that hum of the perpetual present that many believe to be the affective tenor of postmodernity itself.

Perhaps, then, we could say that *Breaking Bad* lies between the cinema that once was, and the television to come. And so we return to that idea, proffered in the introduction, of the cinematic as a flickering across the moving-image landscape: the cinematic as always a pure potentiality, waiting to be unfolded. There is a perfect figure for this at the very end of the cooking montage set to the Monkees' "Goin' Down" in episode 507 ("Say My Name"): a time-lapse image of the Albuquerque landscape from late afternoon to night, where finally in the starry night sky we see at frame right a star brighter than all the rest flashing upward from behind the mountains (fig. 5.14). It appears for only a moment, and then the scene fades out.

While we could search for cosmic interpretations of this perhaps accidental flickering of light in the frame, what I immediately thought of when I first saw it was yet another spectral haunting from the film archive: when the overhead view of the nocturnal Chicago cityscape is suddenly punctuated by a spark from the tracks of the L train in *Risky Business* (Paul Brickman, 1983). Released when the Reagan and Thatcher administrations were overseeing the early moves toward privatization of

5.14. A star flashes

what before was considered the commons, *Risky Business* offers a veritable portrait of the ethos of the neoliberal regime in its emergence: the entrepreneurial curation of the self, prostitution as the general equivalent of capitalism. By the time of *Breaking Bad*, this regime is in full dominance, and it is a fundamental starting point for understanding the industrial, technological, and aesthetic shifts that have occurred in twenty-first-century dramatic television. I have shown how an attention to the cinematic can enable us to enlarge our understanding of the meaning of this singular conjuncture. But even more important, what the cinematic in *Breaking Bad* can make us realize is that the riskiest business of all would be our attempt to break our addiction to that most dangerous of drugs—ourselves—which, as Walter Benjamin so beautifully put it, we take in solitude.[15]

Notes

Introduction

1. Kevin Jagernauth, "Before 'Breaking Bad' This Weekend, Watch Extensive Q&As with Bryan Cranston, Vince Gilligan, Bob Odenkirk & More," *IndieWire*, August 8, 2013, http://blogs.indiewire.com/theplaylist/before-breaking-bad-this-weekend-watch-extensive-q-as-with-bryan-cranston-vince-gilligan-bob-odenkirk-more-20130808.

2. Spigel, *TV by Design*. On the *Point of View* series, see 171–72.

3. Martin, *Difficult Men*, 154.

4. Steven Zeitchik, "Out of the Box: Lines between TV and Film Vanishing," *Chicago Tribune*, May 22, 2016.

5. Lynn Spigel, introduction to Spigel and Olsson, *Television after TV*, 2, 6.

6. Good starting points for understanding the interaction of these factors would be Spigel and Olsson, *Television after TV*, and Lotz, *The Television Will Be Revolutionized*. For an excellent overview of the history of HBO, see Santo, "Para-television and Discourses of Distinction." For an excellent journalistic account of the factors driving contemporary "quality television," see Martin, *Difficult Men*.

7. Zborowski, "The Presentation of Detail and the Organization of Time in *The Royle Family*," 132. The essays on comedy compose part 2 of this collection; notable among them are Clayton, "Why Comedy Is at Home on Television," and Diaz Branco, "Situating Comedy." Some more recent essays of note include Logan, "'Quality Television' as a Critical Obstacle," and Vermeulen and Rustad, "Watching Television with Jacques Rancière."

8. Gray and Lotz, *Television Studies*, 53.

9. For an overview of these arguments, see Mills, "What Does It Mean to Call Television 'Cinematic'?," and Jaramillo, "Rescuing Television from 'the Cinematic.'"

10. For an excellent discussion of the history of AMC's programming and business models, see Jaramillo, "AMC."

11. Keeling, *The Witch's Flight*, 3.

12. See Lacan, *Seminar XI*, 32; also the "sardine can incident," 95.

13. I am thus aligning myself with what might be called the aesthetic turn in recent philosophy: in this turn, Kant's Third Critique moves to center stage and in a sense becomes the "logical prerequisite" of the earlier two critiques. As Steven Shaviro puts it, "Understanding and morality alike must therefore be subordinated to aesthetics. It is only after the subject has constructed or synthesized itself out of its feelings, out of its encounters with the world, that it can then go on to understand that world—or to change it." Shaviro, *Without Criteria*, loc. 516–22.

14. This narrative structures much of Brett Martin's *Difficult Men*; see also Lotz, *Cable Guys*, and Jaramillo, "AMC." For a superb essay that links the industrial, the economic, the cultural, and the textual, see Szalay, "The Writer as Producer; or, The Hip Figure after HBO."

15. Julia Leyda has done excellent work on neoliberal financialization and the white male in *Breaking Bad*. See Leyda, "*Breaking Bad*" and "The Financialization of Domestic Space in *Arrested Development* and *Breaking Bad*." See also Pierson, "Breaking Neoliberal?," and Faucette, "Taking Control."

16. Exemplary here is Reding, *Methland*.

17. At the time of writing, the drug crisis has shifted away from meth and toward opioid addiction. It wouldn't be a stretch, though, to argue that this simply marks the next "moment" in the evolution of the precarity of the laboring classes, the moment in which they simply give up. In the *MSNBC News* segment "One Nation Overdosed: Ohio County Becomes Epicenter of Opioid Epidemic," the sheriff of Montgomery County, Ohio, comments that people are depressed and "self-medicating." *MSNBC News*, June 19, 2017, http://www.msnbc.com/msnbc-news/watch/ohio-county-becomes-epicenter-of-opioid-epidemic-971103299930.

18. Pierson, *"Breaking Bad"*; from a more American studies angle, Wanat and Engel, *Breaking Down "Breaking Bad"*; finally, Blevins and Wood, *The Methods of "Breaking Bad."*

19. Ray, *A Certain Tendency of the Hollywood Cinema*, esp. chaps. 9 and 10.

20. In the *New York Times*, David Segal speculated whether *Breaking Bad*'s creator, Vince Gilligan, might be television's first "red state auteur." David Segal, "The Dark Art of Breaking Bad," *New York Times*, July 6, 2011.

21. Mittell, "Narrative Complexity in Contemporary American Television," 35.

22. Miller, "Anal *Rope*," 119–22, 126.

23. Mittell, "The Qualities of Complexity," esp. 49–50.

24. Logan, *"Breaking Bad" and Dignity*, 3.

25. This is a project also shared by Sean O'Sullivan. See O'Sullivan, "Broken on Purpose."

26. This tradition includes V. F. Perkins, Stanley Cavell, William Rothman, and Gilberto Perez, all of whom he engages with in his introduction.

27. Bordwell, *The Way Hollywood Tells It*.

28. The notion that cinema works to reprogram the human sensorium is implicit in the title of Miriam Hansen's essay "The Mass Production of the Senses." See also Hansen, *Cinema and Experience*, especially the many sections on play and the mimetic faculty.

29. Since the late 1990s, there has been an explosion of work in the humanities on affect, more than I can do justice to in an endnote. In terms of how I will be developing the concept in this book, key reference points—aside from Gilles Deleuze's lectures on Spinoza—are Brinkema, *The Forms of the Affects*; Shaviro, *Post-cinematic Affect*; and Berlant, *Cruel Optimism*. Deleuze's university lectures on Spinoza are available in English at "Lectures by Gilles Deleuze," February 2007, http://deleuzelectures.blogspot.com/2007/02/on-spinoza.html.

30. Panagia, *The Political Life of Sensation*, 11–16.

31. The "straight corridor" is the metaphor David Bordwell uses to characterize classical Hollywood's formal system, providing a template for "the way Hollywood tells it"; Bordwell, "Classical Hollywood Cinema," 18–26. My discussion of the self-consciousness of *Breaking Bad*'s formal devices is grounded in the tradition in modernist criticism that tells us that the work of art teaches us how we are to understand it.

32. Paul MacInnes, "Breaking Bad Creator Vince Gilligan: The Man Who Turned Walter White from Mr Chips to Scarface," *Guardian*, May 18, 2012, https://www.theguardian.com/tv-and-radio/2012/may/19/vince-gilligan-breaking-bad.

33. This episode has been analyzed by Jeffrey R. Di Leo in "Flies in the Marketplace."

34. By suggesting that *Breaking Bad* is not operating in the mode of blank parody, I am decidedly not rejecting Fredric Jameson's characterization of postmodernism as a cultural logic, a schema that will be mobilized in several places later in this book. Jameson, "Postmodernism, or The Cultural Logic of Late Capitalism." To say that pastiche is one manifestation of the cultural logic that is postmodernism is not to say that it is invariably found everywhere; I

would argue that the best reading of Jameson sees the relation between cultural logics and relations of production as malleable, shifting, and supple.

35. See Miller, "Anal *Rope*," 125–26.

Chapter 1. The Cinematic

1. See, for example, Kackman, "Quality Television, Melodrama, and Cultural Complexity"; Santo, "Para-television and Discourses of Distinction"; Jaramillo, "Rescuing Television from 'the Cinematic.'"

2. Sanders, *Miami Vice*; Caldwell, *Televisuality*; Ellis, *Visible Fictions*.

3. For Caldwell's chart, see *Televisuality*, 14 and environs.

4. Caldwell, *Televisuality*, 12.

5. The pioneering work that brought this idea to the English-speaking film world was Andrew Sarris's *The American Cinema*. In 1975, David Thomson created a less laconic, more expansively presented dictionary of directorial styles and worlds in his *Biographical Dictionary of Film*. Interestingly, Thomson is the editor of the "official" *Breaking Bad* book, in the acknowledgments to which Vince Gilligan writes, "*A Biographical Dictionary of Film* has been on the coffee table in front of my television for the past twenty years." Thomson, "*Breaking Bad*," 216.

6. This was the major achievement of, for example, Robin Wood's *Hitchcock's Films*, which used the very aesthetic criteria his mentor F. R. Leavis championed for the great tradition of the English novel to make Hitchcock an object worthy of study in literature departments.

7. François Truffaut's attack on the *cinéma de papa* in "A Certain Tendency in French Cinema," originally published in *Cahiers du Cinéma* in 1954, is the most overt example of this in film studies.

8. Williams, *Television*.

9. See, for example, the collection *The Aesthetics of Cultural Studies*, edited by Michael Bérubé, which seems to promise to bring them together, but most of whose essays adopt an extremely reductive view of aesthetics.

10. Keeling, *The Witch's Flight*, 3.

11. Film scholars might object that I am leaving out Jean Epstein and other earlier theorists who developed a concept of the cinematic connected to *photogénie*. These writers were concerned to differentiate the cinema from the other arts, in the name of medium specificity. But I would argue that for the "young Turks" at *Cahiers* in the 1950s, the issue was not so much to uphold some standard of purity as it was to overturn an outmoded set of practices in the interest of *modernizing* the cinema: which they did, as directors in the New Wave. In this context, it would be especially revealing to return to

Dudley Andrew's essay on *Jules and Jim* (François Truffaut, 1962), where he argues that Catherine's association with a dangerous liquidity can be seen as Truffaut's (and the New Wave's) anxiety over the televisual flows newly entering the audiovisual landscape. See Andrew, "Jules, Jim, and Walter Benjamin." See also Tweedie, *The Age of New Waves*, esp. chap. 1.

12. The *politique* in the *politique des auteurs*, mistranslated by Sarris as "theory," in its more accurate translation as "policy" helps resolve some of the contradictions inhering in the idea of film authorship. For a good elaboration on thematics vs. visual organization, see Perkins, *Film as Film*.

13. Bordwell, Staiger, and Thompson, *Classical Hollywood Cinema*, esp. chap. 1.

14. See the sections on Hollywood cinema in Hillier, *Cahiers du Cinéma*.

15. Vince Gilligan, interview with Peter Guber and Peter Bart on *AMC Shootout*, included on the extras for *Breaking Bad: The Complete First Season*, Blu-ray (Sony Pictures Television, 2008).

16. The Internet Movie Database gives the budget as $6 million, a figure confirmed by *Vanity Fair*, which gives the original proposed budget as $2.5 million. But even after this near 250 percent increase, *The Godfather*'s budget was half that of the A-list picture *Man of La Mancha* (Arthur Hiller, 1972). See Mark Seal, "The Godfather Wars," *Vanity Fair*, February 4, 2009, https://www.vanityfair.com/news/2009/03/godfather200903.

17. Martin, *Mise en Scène and Film Style*, 24–27.

18. For a contemporary discussion of resonance and action-at-a-distance, see Restivo, "Wong Kar-wai," 140–42.

19. Casey Cipriani, "On 'Breaking Bad' Regrets, When Walt Turned Bad and a Surprising Guest Role: 10 Highlights from Vince Gilligan's MoMI Talks with Charlie Rose," *IndieWire*, July 29, 2013, http://www.indiewire.com/article/television/breaking-bad-momi-event.

20. Thomas Elsaesser gives an exemplary account of this critical tradition in U.S. film melodrama in his "Tales of Sound and Fury."

21. Vince Gilligan, commentary, episode 101 ("Pilot"), *Breaking Bad: The Complete First Season*, Blu-ray. See also Brett Martin, "Inside the Breaking Bad Writers' Room: How Vince Gilligan Runs the Show," *Guardian*, September 20, 2013, https://www.theguardian.com/tv-and-radio/2013/sep/20/breaking-bad-writers-room-vince-gilligan, in which Gilligan calls the auteur theory a "load of horseshit."

22. Deleuze, *Cinema 1* and *Cinema 2*; Simondon, *Imagination et invention*; Mitchell, *What Do Pictures Want?*; Rancière, *The Future of the Image*; Väliaho, *Biopolitical Screens*.

23. Väliaho, *Biopolitical Screens*, 93, italics mine.

24. See Ross, *Fast Cars, Clean Bodies*; also Restivo, *The Cinema of Economic Miracles*. For television's relation to the postwar reorganization of space and everyday life, the key work is Spigel, *Make Room for TV*.

25. The notion of life as increasingly moving toward a condition of generalized warfare was initially articulated in film studies by cultural psychoanalysis (Joan Copjec, Slavoj Žižek) following arguments by Jacques Lacan. The accuracy of this assessment can be verified today by simply looking at the comments section of just about any website. The idea has also gained traction via work on the relationships between military technology and video gaming. See, for example, Väliaho, *Biopolitical Screens*.

26. Bryan Cranston, who directed the episode, credited special-effects person Dennis Petersen with rigging up the stack of cars. Commentary, episode 201 ("Seven Thirty-Seven"), *Breaking Bad: The Complete Second Season*, Blu-ray (Sony Pictures Television, 2009).

27. The body of work on cinema and affect is large and growing, but the connection being made here to mise-en-scène has not been a central focus of that work, even though I would argue that this connection implicitly underwrites the first moves of Deleuze in the cinema books, via his notions of "ensembles" and "mobile sets." Deleuze, *Cinema 1*, chap. 2.

28. Rancière here is simply using for his own ends the notion of image developed by Deleuze in the cinema books, a notion that comes out of a reading of Henri-Louis Bergson. See Deleuze, *Cinema 1*, 56–60.

29. Rancière, *Bela Tarr*, 65–66. See also Panagia, *The Political Life of Sensation*, 11–20, for a development of the concept of "narratocracy."

30. Dana Polan has identified the ways that *The Sopranos* brings in techniques from the Italian art cinema of the 1960s. Polan, *The Sopranos*, 88–89.

31. Rancière, *Bela Tarr*, 8.

32. Bazin, *What Is Cinema?*, 1:42.

33. See Miriam Hansen's reading of Walter Benjamin's work on cinema, especially the sections on play and *spielraum*, in *Cinema and Experience*, esp. 190–204.

34. Director of photography John Slovis, in the commentary to episode 309 ("Kafkaesque"), talks about wanting to produce "expressive shots" rather than just presenting the story, thus implicitly making this distinction between the image and the narrative. He notes, "You want cinematic pacing rather than just cutting to dialogue." *Breaking Bad: The Complete Third Season*, Blu-ray (Sony Pictures Television, 2010).

35. There have been a few essays on Werner Heisenberg in relation to *Breaking Bad*, including Brodesco, "Heisenberg, Epistemological Implications of a Criminal Pseudonym," and Poe, "Patriarchy and the 'Heisenberg Principle.'"

36. For discussions of the cold openings of *Breaking Bad*, see Sanchez-Baro, "Uncertain Beginnings," and Logan, "Flash Forwards in *Breaking Bad*."

37. "Breaking Bad Interview with Bryan Cranston, Aaron Paul, and Vince Gilligan," YouTube, posted February 12, 2014, https://www.youtube.com/watch?v=XRRwURiX9R8.

38. Bazin, *What Is Cinema?*, 2:28.

39. On neoliberal economies, see especially Marazzi, *Capital and Affects*; Väliaho, *Biopolitical Screens*; Berlant, *Cruel Optimism*.

Chapter 2. The House

1. The use of handheld cameras is discussed by the production personnel in the commentaries to episodes 312 ("Half Measures") and 408 ("Hermanos"). *Breaking Bad: The Complete Third Season*, Blu-ray (Sony Pictures Television, 2010); *Breaking Bad: The Complete Fourth Season*, Blu-ray (Sony Pictures Television, 2011).

2. Benjamin, "The Work of Art in the Age of Its Technological Reproducibility," 117.

3. Jacques Derrida, "Artifactualities," in Derrida and Stiegler, *Echographies of Television*, 1–27.

4. See Gwynne Watkins, "The Breaking Bad GQ+A: Production Designer Mark Freeborn Details the Transformation of Walter White's House" (interview), *GQ*, August 19, 2013, www.gq.com/story/the-breaking-bad-gqa-production-designer-mark-freeborn-details-the-transformation-of-walter-whites-h.

5. "The Sets of *Breaking Bad*," *Breaking Bad: The Complete Fourth Season*, Blu-ray.

6. "The White House Tour," *Breaking Bad: The Complete Fourth Season*, Blu-ray.

7. Discussion boards at breakingbad.wikia.com, accessed January 21, 2016. I am unable to retrieve this thread from the wiki; it will not come up on a search.

8. It isn't exactly a crane shot. As episode director Scott Winant explains, use of a crane was impossible given the space, so the camera was raised by a machine hoist, which is why the image appears to be shaking or swaying during the movement upward. Commentary, episode 411 ("Crawl Space"), *Breaking Bad: The Complete Fourth Season*, Blu-ray.

9. Brooks, *The Melodramatic Imagination*, 9.

10. The connection between the serial narratives of television and melodrama is discussed by Linda Williams in *On "The Wire,"* 49–50.

11. Newman, "From Beats to Arcs," 18–19.

12. Williams, *On "The Wire,"* 64–76.

13. When attempting to do this type of beat analysis on several episodes of *Breaking Bad*, my grad assistant Christopher Minz and I felt repeatedly thwarted by the unique organizational structures of the series. For example, the organization of a cold opening—itself seemingly a discrete unit—by the unfolding of a single idea, even when it contains, say, a flashback to a different space-time block. Or the unfolding of one line of dramatic action across several distinct locales in one house. For this reason, we didn't calculate averages. Still, the beat lasting, say, one minute and some seconds (the average Williams found for *The Wire*) tended to be the shortest beats in any given episode of *Breaking Bad*. Every episode we looked at had more than one beat clocking near three minutes, and each had at least one beat coming in at over five minutes. There are many instances of beats of extremely long duration: the flashback to the Eladio compound, where Max is murdered, runs over eleven minutes. The scene where Hank and Gomez arrest Walt in the desert runs nearly twelve minutes, though broken up into three "minibeats": Walt's surrender, Hank's phone call to Marie, and the arrival of the neo-Nazis.

14. Elsaesser, "Tales of Sound and Fury," 173–75.

15. For recent reconsiderations of televisual duration, see, for example, Diaz Branco, "Situating Comedy," 94–96.

16. This is how Deborah L. Jaramillo characterizes the arguments supporting cinematic television (though the quotes here are my scare quotes, not citations from her essay). Jaramillo, "Rescuing Television from 'the Cinematic,'" 68–71.

17. See Diaz Branco, "Situating Comedy."

18. Villarejo, *Ethereal Queer*, 80.

19. Villarejo, *Ethereal Queer*, 154.

20. Zarzosa, *Refiguring Melodrama in Film and Television*, chap. 2.

21. Elsaesser, "Tales of Sound and Fury," 186–88.

22. That the *Godfather* films were central reference points for the writers and creative personnel on *Breaking Bad* is clear from the paratexts of the series, especially the *Breaking Bad* Insider podcast hosted by editor Kelley Dixon.

23. Zarzosa, *Refiguring Melodrama in Film and Television*, chap. 2, esp. 38–39.

24. Zarzosa, *Refiguring Melodrama in Film and Television*, 41; Deleuze, *Cinema 1*, 111–22.

25. Williams, *On "The Wire,"* 113–14.

26. In the introduction, I discussed Robert Ray's elaboration of left and right cycles in *A Certain Tendency of the Hollywood Cinema*.

Chapter 3. The Puzzle

1. For a summary of the interpretative strategies around the Hitchcockian object, see Restivo, "Hitchcock and the Postmodern," 558–61.

2. Deleuze, *Cinema 1*, 203–4.

3. See Kogonada, "Breaking Bad // POV," Vimeo, posted January 9, 2012, https://vimeo.com/34773713.

4. Benjamin, "Surrealism"; the "last" in the subtitle is to be taken in the sense of the French *actuel*, "latest" or "current."

5. Benjamin, "Surrealism," 210.

6. Benjamin, "Surrealism," 210.

7. Jameson, "Postmodernism, or The Cultural Logic of Late Capitalism," 59–62, 66–68.

8. Jennifer Kingson, "A Brief History of Chemistry Sets," *New York Times*, December 25, 2012; Sarah Zielinski, "The Rise and Fall of the Chemistry Set," *Smithsonian*, October 10, 2012, https://www.smithsonianmag.com/science-nature/the-rise-and-fall-and-rise-of-the-chemistry-set-70359831/.

9. Benjamin, "Surrealism," 213.

10. Edelman, *No Future*, 4, 17, 27; Benjamin, "Surrealism," 216.

11. For an excellent discussion of the surrealism essay and Benjamin's notions of image- and body-space, see Hansen, *Cinema and Experience*, 140 and following.

12. Benjamin, "The Work of Art in the Age of Its Technological Reproducibility," 112.

13. Benjamin, "Surrealism," 218.

14. Miriam Hansen nevertheless does an excellent job trying to unpack the notion. See Hansen, *Cinema and Experience*, 144, 169.

15. This technique is discussed by Dafydd Wood in the context of the formalist procedure of defamiliarization. Wood, "Flies and One-Eyed Bears," loc. 355–75.

16. Deleuze, *Cinema 2*, 68–69.

17. Deleuze, *Cinema 2*, 130–31.

18. Deleuze, *Cinema 2*, 81: "We see in the crystal the perpetual foundation of time, non-chronological time. . . . This is the powerful, non-organic Life that grips the world"; Bennett, *Vibrant Matter*.

Chapter 4. Just Gaming

1. The writers and actors were well aware of the meta quality of the card-playing rehearsal. They use that very word to describe it in the commentary

to episode 404 ("Bullet Points"). *Breaking Bad: The Complete Fourth Season*, Blu-ray (Sony Pictures Television, 2011).

2. Lyotard and Thébaud, *Just Gaming*, 16–18.

3. Lyotard, *The Postmodern Condition*, 3–10.

4. Lyotard, *Differend*, preface and passim.

5. See Doane, "Information, Crisis, Catastrophe," and Mellencamp, "TV Time and Catastrophe, or *Beyond the Pleasure Principle* of Television."

6. Derrida and Stiegler, *Echographies of Television*.

7. See Edelman, *No Future*, chap. 1.

8. Bauman, *Liquid Modernity*, 4.

9. Massumi, *The Power at the End of the Economy*, 114n2, 22.

10. Massumi, *The Power at the End of the Economy*, 22. Coincidentally, as I was putting final touches on the manuscript of this chapter, it was announced that Richard H. Thaler would receive the 2017 Nobel Prize in economics. In his book *Misbehaving: The Making of Behavioral Economics*, he makes a similar critique of the rational subject presumed by mainstream economics today, though certainly he is not situating his work in relation to Foucault, Deleuze, or the radical tradition Massumi links to. In fact, Thaler would no doubt disagree with my inclusion of Adam Smith in the genealogy of the "rational" economic subject, as Thaler continually reminds us that before *The Wealth of Nations*, Smith wrote a study of the "passions." However, since neoliberal economists often present their model of the rational subject as deriving from Smith, I let the passage stand as is.

11. Michel Foucault, preface to Deleuze and Guattari, *Anti-Oedipus*, xv–xvi.

12. Among the many "mythbusting" analyses of the chemistry in the series, see William Herkewitz, "Breaking Bad Fact vs Fiction: Walter White's Secret Formula," *Popular Mechanics*, August 19, 2013, http://www.popularmechanics.com/culture/tv/a9386/breaking-bad-fact-vs-fiction-walter-whites-secret-formula-15826137/.

Chapter 5. Immanence: A Life

1. Amy Villarejo has seen this happen, for example, in the event of the broadcast of the Loud family saga in the 1970s. As she notes, the time the series presented us with "was also television time, or rather times: a mesh of temporalities of real life, recording, transmission, repetition, and seriality in which . . . we all live." Villarejo, *Ethereal Queer*, 118.

2. The Breaking Bad Wiki describes the action thusly: "At his last dying minute, he braces himself on a tank with a bloody hand, leaving a vaguely W-shaped blood red smear print on the shiny stainless steel surface, as the

reflection of tears and the smile on his face drop down, as he falls to the floor. Flat on his back, his lasts moments amongst his beloved lab equipment, content with his last love being for what he made expertly, and what he felt alive for as Heisenberg. Knowing that his family is safe and financially secure, Walt dies serenely." Is the blood stain a *W*, a mark of the life of an individual? Or is it a smear, marking simply "a" life? Notice how once the *W* makes its appearance, the author is able to sneak in all sorts of ungrounded claims about Walt's mental state as he dies. "Felina," Summary, Breaking Bad Wiki, accessed April 24, 2018, http://breakingbad.wikia.com/wiki/Felina.

3. Deleuze, "Immanence: A Life." Michael Hardt has an excellent discussion of this essay in his lecture notes for *A Thousand Plateaus*, available online at http://people.duke.edu/~hardt/mp6.htm.

4. Deleuze develops this notion of vantage point in his early book on Proust, *Proust and Signs*, 106, 136.

5. In order to get the downward-looking tracking shot, the floor of the loft above was cut through along the path the camera would follow.

6. See Delany, *Times Square Red, Times Square Blue*.

7. For an excellent discussion of cinematic mappings of New York City in the mid-1970s, see Toscano and Kinkle, *Cartographies of the Absolute*, 105–36. On left and right cycles, see Ray, *A Certain Tendency of the Hollywood Cinema*. Fredric Jameson's brilliant allegorical reading of *Dog Day Afternoon* should also be mentioned here: Jameson notes the way the film indexes the shift I am talking about via its juxtaposition of the neighborhood branch bank (as "outpost" of the center of financialization) with the group of onlookers outside, chanting, "Attica! Attica!" Jameson, "Class and Allegory in Contemporary Mass Culture."

8. The concept of "a life" has interesting connections to the Freudian unconscious (and its "flickering" as I described it in the introduction to this book), though I have not seen this idea developed anywhere.

9. Shaviro, *Without Criteria*. On the aesthetic turn in recent theory, see introduction, note 13.

10. Sedgwick notes that these circulating objects "seemed to have functioned as badges of homosexual recognition." Sedgwick, *Between Men*, 206.

11. Champagne, "Walt Whitman, Our Great Gay Poet?," 652–54, 660. While Champagne doesn't mention Deleuze and Guattari, a strong connection can be made here to their distinction between the arborescent and the rhizomatic: traditional thought, with its treelike organization, its branching chains of binary oppositions and its hierarchical structure, fixes us into defined and pregiven categories; rhizomatic thought propagates connections at a distance, improbable linkages through underground shoots, and resembles more the

nonhierarchical nodal structure of a network. See Deleuze and Guattari, *A Thousand Plateaus*, chap. 1.

12. Lawrence, "Whitman," 150, 151, 157. Here again with Lawrence, we can see how Whitman's subversion of hierarchies in his lists of incommensurable things brings to mind the first great moves in Deleuze and Guattari's *Anti-Oedipus*, where the desiring-machines join together in a connective synthesis. Before there are defined objects with boundaries, before there are individuals with identities, before there are even logical relations, there are partial objects linked together promiscuously by the connective "and." Deleuze and Guattari, *Anti-Oedipus*, chap. 1.

13. On the restoration of belief in this world, see Deleuze, *Cinema 2*, 170–73.

14. This "music video" likely antedates the form as it established itself in the 1970s. Most likely it was a promo reel made to accompany the album, though I cannot ascertain its source. See "Tommy James & The Shondells—Crystal Blue Persuasion—1969," YouTube, posted September 28, 2010, https://www.youtube.com/watch?v=XDl8ZPm3GrU.

15. Benjamin, "Surrealism," 216.

Bibliography

Andrew, Dudley. "Jules, Jim, and Walter Benjamin." In *The Image in Dispute: Art and Cinema in the Age of Photography*, ed. Dudley Andrew, 33–54. Austin: University of Texas Press, 1997.

Bauman, Zygmunt. *Liquid Modernity*. Cambridge: Polity, 2000.

Bazin, André. *What Is Cinema?* 2 vols. Berkeley: University of California Press, 1972.

Benjamin, Walter. "Surrealism: Last Snapshot of the European Intelligentsia." In *Selected Writings*, vol. 2, part 1, *1927–1930*, ed. Michael W. Jennings, Howard Eiland, and Gary Smith, trans. Rodney Livingstone, 207–21. Cambridge, MA: Harvard University Press, 1999.

Benjamin, Walter. "The Work of Art in the Age of Its Technological Reproducibility" (second version). In *Selected Writings*, vol. 3., ed. Howard Eiland and Michael Jennings, trans. Edmund Jephcott et al., 101–33. Cambridge, MA: Harvard University Press, 2002.

Bennett, Jane. *Vibrant Matter: A Political Ecology of Things*. Durham, NC: Duke University Press, 2010.

Berlant, Lauren. *Cruel Optimism*. Durham, NC: Duke University Press, 2011.

Bérubé, Michael, ed. *The Aesthetics of Cultural Studies*. Malden, MA: Blackwell, 2005.

Blevins, Jacob, and Dafydd Wood, eds. *The Methods of "Breaking Bad": Essays on Narrative, Character and Ethics*. Jefferson, NC: McFarland, 2015.

Bordwell, David. "Classical Hollywood Cinema: Narrational Principles and Procedures." In *Narrative, Apparatus, Ideology*, ed. Phil Rosen, 17–34. New York: Columbia University Press, 1986.

Bordwell, David. *The Way Hollywood Tells It: Story and Style in Modern Movies*. Berkeley: University of California Press, 2006.

Bordwell, David, Janet Staiger, and Kristin Thompson. *Classical Hollywood*

Cinema: Film Style and Mode of Production to 1960. London: Routledge, 1985.

Brinkema, Eugenie. *The Forms of the Affects*. Durham, NC: Duke University Press, 2014.

Brodesco, Alberto. "Heisenberg, Epistemological Implications of a Criminal Pseudonym." In *"Breaking Bad": Critical Essays on the Contexts, Politics, Style, and Reception of the Television Series*, ed. David P. Pierson, 53–71. Lanham, MD: Lexington Books, 2014.

Brooks, Peter. *The Melodramatic Imagination: Balzac, Henry James, Melodrama, and the Mode of Excess*. New Haven, CT: Yale University Press, 1995.

Caldwell, John T. *Televisuality: Style, Crisis, and Authority in American Television*. New Brunswick, NJ: Rutgers University Press, 1995.

Champagne, John. "Walt Whitman, Our Great Gay Poet?" *Journal of Homosexuality* 55, no. 4 (2008): 648–64.

Clayton, Alex. "Why Comedy Is at Home on Television." In *Television Aesthetics and Style*, ed. Jason Jacobs and Steven Peacock, 79–92. New York: Bloomsbury, 2013.

Delany, Samuel R. *Times Square Red, Times Square Blue*. New York: NYU Press, 1999.

Deleuze, Gilles. *Cinema 1: The Movement Image*. Trans. Hugh Tomlinson and Barbara Habberjam. Minneapolis: University of Minnesota Press, 1986.

Deleuze, Gilles. *Cinema 2: The Time-Image*. Trans. Hugh Tomlinson and Robert Galeta. Minneapolis: University of Minnesota Press, 1989.

Deleuze, Gilles. "Immanence: A Life." In *Pure Immanence: Essays on a Life*. Trans. Anne Boyman, 25–34. New York: Zone Books, 2001.

Deleuze, Gilles. *Proust and Signs*. Trans. Richard Howard. New York: George Braziller, 1972.

Deleuze, Gilles, and Félix Guattari. *Anti-Oedipus: Capitalism and Schizophrenia*. Trans. Robert Hurley, Mark Seem, and Helen R. Lane. Minneapolis: University of Minnesota Press, 1983.

Deleuze, Gilles, and Félix Guattari. *A Thousand Plateaus: Capitalism and Schizophrenia*. Trans. Brian Massumi. Minneapolis: University of Minnesota Press, 1987.

Derrida, Jacques, and Bernard Stiegler. *Echographies of Television*. Trans. Jennifer Bajorek. Cambridge: Polity, 2002.

Diaz Branco, Sérgio. "Situating Comedy: Inhabitation and Duration in Classical American Sitcoms." In *Television Aesthetics and Style*, ed. Jason Jacobs and Steven Peacock, 93–102. New York: Bloomsbury, 2013.

Di Leo, Jeffrey R. "Flies in the Marketplace: Nietzsche and Neoliberalism in

Breaking Bad." In *The Methods of "Breaking Bad": Essays on Narrative, Character and Ethics*, ed. Jacob Blevins and Dafydd Wood, 26–46. Jefferson, NC: McFarland, 2015.

Doane, Mary Ann. "Information, Crisis, Catastrophe." In *Logics of Television: Essays in Cultural Criticism*, ed. Patricia Mellencamp, 222–39. Bloomington: Indiana University Press, 1990.

Edelman, Lee. *No Future: Queer Theory and the Death Drive*. Durham, NC: Duke University Press, 2004.

Ellis, John. *Visible Fictions: Cinema, Television, Video*. London: Routledge, 1982.

Elsaesser, Thomas. "Tales of Sound and Fury: Observations on the Family Melodrama." In *Movies and Methods*, vol. 2., ed. Bill Nichols, 165–89. Berkeley: University of California Press, 1985.

Faucette, Brian. "Taking Control: Male Angst and the Re-emergence of Hegemonic Masculinity in *Breaking Bad*." In *"Breaking Bad": Critical Essays on the Contexts, Politics, Style, and Reception of the Television Series*, ed. David P. Pierson, 73–86. Lanham, MD: Lexington Books, 2014.

Gray, Jonathan, and Amanda D. Lotz. *Television Studies*. Cambridge: Polity, 2012.

Hansen, Miriam. *Cinema and Experience*. Berkeley: University of California Press, 2012.

Hansen, Miriam. "The Mass Production of the Senses: Classical Cinema as Vernacular Modernism." *Modernism/Modernity* 6, no. 2 (1999): 59–77.

Hillier, James, ed. *Cahiers du Cinéma: The 1950s*. Cambridge, MA: Harvard University Press, 1985.

Jacobs, Jason, and Steven Peacock, eds. *Television Aesthetics and Style*. New York: Bloomsbury, 2013.

Jameson, Fredric. "Class and Allegory in Contemporary Mass Culture: *Dog Day Afternoon* as a Political Film." In *Signatures of the Visible*, 35–54. New York: Routledge, 1992.

Jameson, Fredric. "Postmodernism, or The Cultural Logic of Late Capitalism." *New Left Review* I, no. 146 (July–August 1984): 53–92.

Jaramillo, Deborah L. "AMC: Stumbling toward a New Television Canon." *Television & New Media* 14, no. 2 (March 2013): 167–83.

Jaramillo, Deborah L. "Rescuing Television from 'the Cinematic': The Perils of Dismissing Television Style." In *Television Aesthetics and Style*, ed. Jason Jacobs and Steven Peacock, 67–76. New York: Bloomsbury, 2013.

Kackman, Michael. "Quality Television, Melodrama, and Cultural Complexity." *Flow Journal*, March 5, 2010. https://www.flowjournal.org/2010/03/flow-favorites-quality-television-melodrama-and-cultural-complexity-michael-kackman-university-of-texas-austin.

Keeling, Kara. *The Witch's Flight: The Cinematic, the Black Femme, and the Image of Common Sense*. Durham, NC: Duke University Press, 2007.

Lacan, Jacques. *Seminar XI: The Four Fundamental Concepts of Psychoanalysis*. Trans. Alan Sheridan. New York: Norton, 1981.

Lawrence, D. H. "Whitman." In D. H. Lawrence, *Studies in Classic American Literature*, ed. Ezra Greenspan, Lindeth Vasey, and John Worthen, 148–61. Cambridge: Cambridge University Press, 2003.

Leverette, Marc, Brian L. Ott, and Cara Louise Buckley, eds. *It's Not TV: Watching HBO in the Post-television Era*. New York: Routledge, 2008.

Leyda, Julia. "*Breaking Bad*: A Recessionary Western." In *Violence and Open Spaces: The Subversion of Boundaries and the Transformation of the Western Genre*, ed. Stefanie Müller, Christa Buschendorf, and Katja Sarkowsky, 187–200. Heidelberg: Universitätsverlag Winter, 2017.

Leyda, Julia. "The Financialization of Domestic Space in *Arrested Development* and *Breaking Bad*." In *Class Divisions in Serial Television*, ed. Wibke Schniedermann and Sieglinde Lemke, 159–76. London: Palgrave-Macmillan, 2016.

Logan, Elliott. *"Breaking Bad" and Dignity: Unity and Fragmentation in the Serial Television Drama*. London: Palgrave, 2016.

Logan, Elliott. "Flash Forwards in *Breaking Bad*." In *Television Aesthetics and Style*, ed. Jason Jacobs and Steven Peacock, 219–26. New York: Bloomsbury, 2013.

Logan, Elliott. "'Quality Television' as a Critical Obstacle: Explanation and Aesthetics in Television Studies." *Screen* 57, no. 2 (summer 2016): 144–62.

Lotz, Amanda. *Cable Guys: Television and Masculinities in the 21st Century*. New York: NYU Press, 2014.

Lotz, Amanda. *The Television Will Be Revolutionized*. New York: NYU Press, 2007.

Lyotard, Jean-François. *Differend: Phrases in Dispute*. Trans. Georges Van den Abbeele. Minneapolis: University of Minnesota Press, 1989.

Lyotard, Jean-François. *The Postmodern Condition: A Report on Knowledge*. Trans. Geoff Bennington and Brian Massumi. Minneapolis: University of Minnesota Press, 1984.

Lyotard, Jean-François, and Jean-Loup Thébaud. *Just Gaming*. Trans. Wlad Godzich. Minneapolis: University of Minnesota Press, 1985.

Marazzi, Christian. *Capital and Affects: The Politics of the Language Economy*. Trans. Giuseppina Mecchia. Los Angeles: Semiotext(e), 2011.

Martin, Adrian. *Mise en Scène and Film Style: From Classical Hollywood to New Media Art*. London: Palgrave, 2014.

Martin, Brett. *Difficult Men: Behind the Scenes of a Creative Revolution: From*

"The Sopranos" and "The Wire" to "Mad Men" and "Breaking Bad." New York: Penguin Books, 2013.

Massumi, Brian. *The Power at the End of the Economy*. Durham, NC: Duke University Press, 2015.

Mellencamp, Patricia. "TV Time and Catastrophe, or *Beyond the Pleasure Principle* of Television." In *Logics of Television: Essays in Cultural Criticism*, ed. Patricia Mellencamp, 240–66. Bloomington: Indiana University Press, 1990.

Miller, D. A. "Anal *Rope*." In *Inside Out: Lesbian Theories, Gay Theories*, ed. Diana Fuss, 119–41. New York: Routledge, 1991.

Mills, Brett. "What Does It Mean to Call Television 'Cinematic'?" In *Television Aesthetics and Style*, ed. Jason Jacobs and Steven Peacock, 57–66. New York: Bloomsbury, 2013.

Mitchell, W. J. T. *What Do Pictures Want? The Lives and Loves of Images*. Chicago: University of Chicago Press, 2005.

Mittell, Jason. "Narrative Complexity in Contemporary American Television." *Velvet Light Trap: A Critical Journal of Film & Television*, no. 58 (fall 2006): 29–40.

Mittell, Jason. "The Qualities of Complexity: Vast vs. Dense Seriality in Contemporary Television." In *Television Aesthetics and Style*, ed. Jason Jacobs and Steven Peacock, 45–56. New York: Bloomsbury, 2013.

Newman, Michael Z. "From Beats to Arcs: Toward a Poetics of Television Narrative." *Velvet Light Trap: A Critical Journal of Film & Television*, no. 58 (fall 2006): 16–28.

O'Sullivan, Sean. "Broken on Purpose: Poetry, Serial Television, and the Season." *StoryWorlds: A Journal of Narrative Studies* 2 (2010): 59–77.

Panagia, Davide. *The Political Life of Sensation*. Durham, NC: Duke University Press, 2009.

Perkins, V. F. *Film as Film: Understanding and Judging Movies*. New York: Penguin, 1972.

Pierson, David P., ed. *"Breaking Bad": Critical Essays on the Contexts, Politics, Style, and Reception of the Television Series*. Lanham, MD: Lexington Books, 2014.

Pierson, David P. "Breaking Neoliberal? Neoliberalism, Its Discourses, and *Breaking Bad*." In *"Breaking Bad": Critical Essays on the Contexts, Politics, Style, and Reception of the Television Series*, ed. David P. Pierson, 15–32. Lanham, MD: Lexington Books, 2014.

Poe, Philip. "Patriarchy and the 'Heisenberg Principle.'" In *The Methods of "Breaking Bad": Essays on Narrative, Character and Ethics*, ed. Jacob Blevins and Dafydd Wood, 109–21. Jefferson, NC: McFarland, 2015.

Polan, Dana. *The Sopranos*. Durham, NC: Duke University Press, 2009.
Rancière, Jacques. *Bela Tarr: The Time After*. Trans. Eric Beranek. Minneapolis: University of Minnesota Press, 2013.
Rancière, Jacques. *The Future of the Image*. Trans. Gregory Elliott. New York: Verso, 2007.
Ray, Robert B. *A Certain Tendency of the Hollywood Cinema, 1930–1980*. Princeton, NJ: Princeton University Press, 1985.
Reding, Nick. *Methland: The Death and Life of an American Small Town*. New York: Bloomsbury, 2009.
Restivo, Angelo. *The Cinema of Economic Miracles: Visuality and Modernization in the Italian Art Film*. Durham, NC: Duke University Press, 2002.
Restivo, Angelo. "Hitchcock and the Postmodern." In *Companion to Alfred Hitchcock*, ed. Thomas Leitch and Leland Poague, 555–71. Malden, MA: Wiley, 2011.
Restivo, Angelo. "Wong Kar-wai: Optics of the Virtual." In *Companion to Wong Kar-wai*, ed. Martha Nochimson, 135–52. Malden, MA: Wiley, 2016.
Ross, Kristin. *Fast Cars, Clean Bodies: Decolonization and the Reordering of French Culture*. Cambridge, MA: MIT Press, 1996.
Sanchez-Baro, Rossend. "Uncertain Beginnings: *Breaking Bad*'s Episodic Openings." In *"Breaking Bad": Critical Essays on the Contexts, Politics, Style, and Reception of the Television Series*, ed. David P. Pierson, 139–54. Lanham, MD: Lexington Books, 2014.
Sanders, Steven. *Miami Vice*. Detroit: Wayne State University Press, 2010.
Santo, Avi. "Para-television and Discourses of Distinction: The Culture of Production at HBO." In *It's Not TV: Watching HBO in the Post-television Era*, ed. Marc Leverette, Brian L. Ott, and Cara Louise Buckley, 19–45. New York: Routledge, 2008.
Sarris, Andrew. *The American Cinema: Directors and Directions, 1929–1968*. New York: Dutton, 1968.
Sedgwick, Eve Kosofsky. *Between Men: English Literature and Male Homosocial Desire*. New York: Columbia University Press, 1985.
Shaviro, Steven. *Post-cinematic Affect*. Winchester, UK: Zero Books, 2010.
Shaviro, Steven. *Without Criteria: Kant, Whitehead, Deleuze, and Aesthetics*. Cambridge, MA: MIT Press, 2012.
Simondon, Gilbert. *Imagination et invention (1965–1966)*. Paris: Presse Universitaires de France, 2014.
Spigel, Lynn. *Make Room for TV: Television and the Family Ideal in Postwar America*. Chicago: University of Chicago Press, 1992.
Spigel, Lynn. *TV by Design: Modern Art and the Rise of Network Television*. Chicago: University of Chicago Press, 2009.

Spigel, Lynn, and Jan Olsson, eds. *Television after TV: Essays on a Medium in Transition*. Durham, NC: Duke University Press, 2004.

Szalay, Michael. "The Writer as Producer; or, The Hip Figure after HBO." In *Mad Men, Mad World: Sex, Politics, Style, and the 1960s*, ed. Lauren M. E. Goodlad, Lilya Kaganovsky, and Robert A. Rushing, 111–29. Durham, NC: Duke University Press, 2013.

Thaler, Richard H. *Misbehaving: The Making of Behavioral Economics*. New York: Norton, 2016.

Thomson, David. *A Biographical Dictionary of Film*. New York: Knopf, 1975.

Thomson, David, ed. *"Breaking Bad": The Official Book*. New York: Sterling / Sony Pictures, 2015.

Toscano, Alberto, and Jeff Kinkle. *Cartographies of the Absolute*. Winchester, UK: Zero Books, 2015.

Truffaut, François. "A Certain Tendency in French Cinema." Trans. Peter Graham. In *The French New Wave: Critical Landmarks*, ed. Peter Graham and Ginette Vincendeau, 39–63. London: British Film Institute, 2009.

Tweedie, James. *The Age of New Waves: Art Cinema and the Staging of Globalization*. New York: Oxford University Press, 2013.

Väliaho, Pasi. *Biopolitical Screens: Image, Power, and the Neoliberal Brain*. Cambridge, MA: MIT Press, 2014.

Vermeulen, Timotheus, and Gry C. Rustad. "Watching Television with Jacques Rancière: US 'Quality Television,' *Mad Men* and the 'Late Cut.'" *Screen* 54, no. 3 (autumn 2013): 341–54.

Villarejo, Amy. *Ethereal Queer: Television, Historicity, Desire*. Durham, NC: Duke University Press, 2014.

Wanat, Matt, and Leonard Engel, eds. *Breaking Down "Breaking Bad": Critical Perspectives*. Albuquerque: University of New Mexico Press, 2016.

Williams, Linda. *On "The Wire."* Durham, NC: Duke University Press, 2014.

Williams, Raymond. *Television: Technology and Cultural Form*. New York: Routledge, 2003. Orig. pub. London: Fontana, 1974.

Wood, Dafydd. "Flies and One-Eyed Bears: The Maturation of a Genre." In *The Methods of "Breaking Bad": Essays on Narrative, Character and Ethics*, ed. Jacob Blevins and Dafydd Wood, 11–25. Jefferson, NC: McFarland, 2015.

Wood, Robin. *Hitchcock's Films*. New York: Barnes, 1965.

Zarzosa, Agustín. *Refiguring Melodrama in Film and Television: Captive Affects, Elastic Sufferings, Vicarious Objects*. Lanham, MD: Lexington Books, 2013.

Zborowski, James. "The Presentation of Detail and the Organization of Time in *The Royle Family*." In *Television Aesthetics and Style*, ed. Jason Jacobs and Steven Peacock, 125–34. New York: Bloomsbury, 2013.

Index

"Abiquiu" (episode 311), 65
"ABQ" (episode 213), 51, 89, 101–2, 104
actions-at-a-distance, 12, 34, 63, 71, 106
actualization (of virtual), 12, 19, 39, 41, 47, 57, 72, 82, 106, 133, 137, 143, 148
Adorno, Theodor, 114
aerial shot, 144
aesthetic event, 7, 120–21
aesthetic experience, 24, 57, 135
aesthetic judgment, 29–30, 38, 65
aesthetics: of art cinema, 43–44, 46–49; creativity and, 149–50, 152–53; criteria and, 7, 150, 160n13, 162n6; Frankfurt School and, 4–5; of horror, 67; and immanence, 98, 100, 114–15; of James Bond films, 129–30; of melodrama, 68–72; and the Open, 153; "operational," 10; and the sensorium, 11, 46, 55, 72, 95–97, 161n28; of spaghetti westerns, 129–32; surrealist, 84–90; television studies and, 29–30
affect: administration of, 56, 136; distribution of forces, 11–12, 43–44; and form, 108, 148, 161n29, 164n27; melodrama and, 70–80; Nietzsche and, 133–34; political, 100, 156; resonance and, 51; and space, 57–61, 66; Spinoza and, 73, 161n29
affirmative culture, 33
allegory, 22, 100, 126, 133
Alphaville (film), 55
AMC, 1, 5, 7
anality, 21–22, 76
Andrea Castillo (character on *Breaking Bad*), 123–24, 148
Andrew, Dudley, 162n11
". . . And the Bag's in the River" (episode 103), 45, 52, 81, 86–88, 119, 125, 132
antihero, 7
archive: of evidence, 100; of images, 2, 24, 36–39, 84, 92, 156
art film, 3, 43–44, 49, 114, 164n30
artifactuality, 56, 121
Assange, Julian, 100
ATM machine, 86, 101
auteur, 3, 7, 30–32, 37
auteur policy, 31
auto graveyard, 39–43, 63, 73, 99

Bacon, Francis, 108
Bad Seed, The (film), 108
Bauman, Zygmunt, 127
Bazin, André, 46, 49
beat (television vs. theater), 68–71, 116, 131, 166n13
Benjamin, Walter: on cinema, 11, 55, 96; on drugs, 92, 95, 157; on the outmoded, 92–94; on the political, 96–99, 114–15, 153–54; on surrealism, 90–99; on the untimely, 94
Bergman, Ingrid, 49, 82
Bigger Than Life (film), 34, 36–37, 39, 68, 93
Big Heat, The (film), 63, 111
"Bit by a Dead Bee" (episode 203), 48
blank parody, 19, 33, 36, 161n34
"Blood Money" (episode 509), 57, 59–60, 102, 108
blue (Walt's "trademark"), 60, 136, 144, 150, 153–54
Bochco, Steven, 27
Bordwell, David, 11, 31, 161n31
bottle episode, 12
bourgeois *intérieur*, 86
"Box Cutter" (episode 401), 123
B-picture, 28. *See also* low budget
Brickman, Paul, 156
Brock Castillo (character on *Breaking Bad*), 124
Brooks, Peter, 68, 70
"Bullet Points" (episode 404), 116–17
Buñuel, Luis, 84
"Buried" (episode 510), 102
"Buyout" (episode 506), 52–54, 84

"Caballo sin Nombre" (episode 302), 59
Cahiers du Cinéma, 11, 162n11
calculability, 113, 118, 135. *See also* futurity
Caldwell, John, 27–28
camera-eye, 70, 80
cancer, 1, 36, 42, 45–46, 81, 90, 116, 119
"Cancer Man" (episode 104), 45, 61, 76, 88–89, 107
capitalism, 6, 30, 40, 74, 92. *See also* neoliberalism
Carrie (film), 53
car wash, 36, 116–17, 122
catastrophe (televised), 120
"Cat's in the Bag . . ." (episode 102), 45, 52–53, 84, 104, 108
Champagne, John, 150–51
Chaplin, Charlie, 6
Chase, David, 3
chemistry, 1, 23, 45, 76, 93–94, 108, 129, 136, 152
chemistry sets, 93–94
chiral, 108, 110
cinemascope, 37
cinematic: and affect, 43, 57, 77, 100; and any-space-whatever, 77–78; and authorship, 30–33, 37–38; debates around, 25–27; in film studies, 6–7, 28–30, 44; as flickering across mediasphere, 6, 156; image archive and, 24, 38–39, 156; as interruptor, 6–7, 11–12, 56, 72, 121; and perception, 6, 11, 54–57, 96, 153–54; vs. televisuality, 27–28, 72; and thresholds, 33, 36; as unfolding, 120. *See also* mise-en-scène
cinematic television: authorship and, 32; as critical problem, 3–5; debates about, 5–6, 26–27; mise-en-scène and, 33, 37; postmodernity and, 56
cinema verité, 6

Citizen Kane (film), 106
classical Hollywood cinema, 14, 19, 28, 46, 60, 73, 96, 130
clichés, 45, 110, 117–18, 133
cold opening. *See* teaser
Cole, Nat King, 125
Colombia, 123
common sense, 6–7, 11, 24, 39, 140
"Confessions" (episode 511), 117
conspiracy, 21, 118
constellation, 114–15. *See also* Benjamin, Walter; Frankfurt School
consumer culture, 41, 86, 98, 133–34. *See also* neoliberalism
Coppola, Francis Ford, 9, 75
Corman, Roger, 95
Cranston, Bryan, 48–49, 128–29
"Crawl Space" (episode 411), 65–67, 147
"Crazy Handful of Nothin'" (episode 106), 45, 62, 129
credit sequence (of *Breaking Bad*), 152–53
Cronenberg, David, 33
"Crystal Blue Persuasion" (song), 154–56
crystal image, 104–13, 167n18
CSI (TV series), 49
Cuba, 40, 61
cultural studies, 30, 72
Czech Republic, 24, 147

Dalí, Salvador, 84
Dallas (TV series), 4
darkroom (photographic), 95–96
DEA, 1, 13, 21–22, 61, 66, 84, 117, 121, 137–38
dead time, 43–44
death drive, 126, 143
death of the author, 38
de Chirico, Giorgio, 88
decision making, 132–34
defamiliarization, 6, 86
deindustrialization, 8. *See also* neoliberalism
Delaney, Samuel, 147
Deleuze, Gilles: affect, 73; any-space-whatever, 77; crystal image, 106–7, 167n18; and the event, 120; life, 142–43; mark/demark, 83; multiplicity, 133; and the Open, 143, 153–54
Deleuze, Gilles, and Félix Guattari, 135; *Anti-Oedipus*, 170n12; *A Thousand Plateaus*, 169n11
De Palma, Brian, 53
Derrida, Jacques, 56, 121
Dickens, Charles, 143
discourse community, 118. *See also* language games
dismemberment, 53–54
distinction, 3, 26, 71. *See also* taste cultures
Dixon, Kelley, 166n22
Dodge Challenger, 44
do-it-yourself culture, 23, 40, 94, 99, 130
domestic space: in films of Nicholas Ray, 35–37, 39; inertia/speed in, 57–58, 77; Jesse's house, 58, 61–62, 77–79, 89; melodrama and, 77; the Schrader house, 58, 60–61; the Schwartz's house, 126–27; and television studies, 68, 70; thresholds in, 62–64; the White house, 57–60, 77, 102, 141
doorknob shot, 49
"Down" (episode 204), 61, 135
Drew Sharp (character on *Breaking Bad*), 52–53, 148

drugs: cartels and, 1, 21; economic precarity and, 8, 96; as escape, 24; as expansion of sensorium, 88, 92, 95–96; heroin, 48–49; marijuana, 45, 61–62, 149; opioids, 160n17; pharmaceuticals, 34–35, 93, 108; as social "issue," 45, 62, 86, 94; subcultures and, 23, 61, 154
dualism, 110–11, 113, 133
DuPont Chemical, 93
duration, 31, 69–72
Dylan, Bob, 13

economic theory, 133–34, 168n10
Edelman, Lee, 96, 126
Edelstein, David, 48
Eladio gang (in *Breaking Bad*), 112, 122
Elliott and Gretchen Schwartz (characters on *Breaking Bad*), 126, 136, 144
Ellis, John, 27
Elsaesser, Thomas, 70, 74
Emilio Koyama (character on *Breaking Bad*), 52, 81, 108, 121
"End Times" (episode 412), 112, 124
ethnic enclave, 21, 24, 125–26, 147
everyday life, 5, 12, 56, 114, 118, 127, 148; administration of, 40; aesthetic rendering of, 37, 46–47; common sense and, 24, 86; as generalized warfare, 41, 141, 164n25
excess, 6, 11, 27, 75, 136
expressionism, 60, 110, 133
extensive relations, 33–35, 37, 153. *See also* intensive relations; narrative

"Face Off" (episode 413), 107, 111–12, 124
family: as criminal enterprise, 23, 124–26; ethnic, 21, 23; fascism and, 135; futurity and, 96; homosexuality and, 23, 151–52; idealized, 19, 90; as inadequate idea, 73–76, 119; melodrama and, 35–36, 61–62, 65, 70, 73–74; middle-class, 7, 21, 126 27; precarity and, 7–8, 36; surrogate, 22, 76, 151–52; televisual, 21, 126–27, 140
fascism (everyday), 135, 154. *See also* nonfascist life
"Felina" (episode 516), 126–27, 140–42, 144–50
feminism, 8
femme fatale, 50
film noir, 51, 60, 63, 67, 101, 107–8, 110–11, 113, 120, 133
Film Society of Lincoln Center, 3
Final Destination 3 (film), 67
flashbacks, 48, 52, 65, 75, 123, 139
flow (televisual), 56, 58, 162n11
fly, 12–14, 19, 38–39
"Fly" (episode 310), 12, 44, 76
Ford, John, 33–34, 102
Foucault, Michel, 133, 135, 148, 150, 154
Frankfurt School, 4, 114
Freeborn, Mark, 57, 67
Freud, Sigmund, 95, 110, 113, 133–34
"Full Measure" (episode 313), 57, 63–64
futurity: and calculability, 118, 135; and the crystal image, 106; and the Open, 148, 156; queer, 126; as transcendental horizon, 96, 97, 115

Gale Boetticher (character on *Breaking Bad*), 14, 23, 63–64, 75–76, 79, 93, 97, 123, 151
gambling, 116–17
gaps (narrative), 7, 46–48
genre, 9, 23, 27, 31, 34, 67–68, 108,

117–18, 123, 130–31. *See also* film noir; left/right cycles (in genres); melodrama; spaghetti western; western
geological time, 131–32, 138, 152–53
geopolitics, 8
Gilligan, Vince, 12, 21, 32, 36–38, 48, 96, 152
Giuliani, Rudy, 147
"Gliding over All" (episode 508), 13–19, 59–60, 76, 121–22, 125, 151, 154
Godard, Jean-Luc, 41, 55, 144
Godfather, The (film), 9, 33, 75, 101, 125, 163n16
"Goin' Down" (song), 156
Goldbergs, The (TV series), 21
golden age, 2–5, 127
Gonzo (character on *Breaking Bad*), 42
Goodfellas (film), 41
GPS, 137–38, 141
Grahame, Gloria, 111
"Granite State" (episode 515), 144
Gray, Jonathan, 5
Gray Matter (in *Breaking Bad*), 126, 135–36
Griffith, D. W., 55
"Grilled" (episode 202), 48
Guattari, Félix. *See* Deleuze, Gilles, and Félix Guattari
Gus Fring (character on *Breaking Bad*): calculation and, 112, 122–24, 134; death of, 107–8, 111–12; as father figure, 23, 65; as a figure of "no future," 126; and homosexuality, 23, 75; and radical evil, 112, 123; relation to Gale, 23, 63

"Half Measures" (episode 312), 48, 107
handheld camera, 27, 54, 70
Hank Schrader (character on *Breaking Bad*), 1, 13, 21, 45, 48, 58–61, 63, 65–66, 75, 84, 116–17, 128, 131, 137–38, 151
Hansen, Miriam, 11
Hardt, Michael, 169n3
haunted images, 2, 19, 24, 96, 102, 111, 144, 156
"Hazard Pay" (episode 503), 88
HBO, 7, 26, 69
Hector "Tio" Salamanca (character on *Breaking Bad*), 111, 123–24
"Heisenberg" (Walter White's street name), 19, 42, 47, 52, 74, 101–2, 117, 153
Heisenberg uncertainty principle, 47
"Hermanos" (episode 408), 86, 123
high school, 1, 8, 36, 62, 76, 108, 149
Hill Street Blues (TV series), 27–28
History of Violence (film), 33
Hitchcock, Alfred, 6, 10, 14, 19, 30–31, 44, 82–83
homelessness, 61
homosexuality, 21, 23, 75, 126, 150–51
homosexual panic, 21
Hostel 2 (film), 67
house style (studio system), 32
Huell Babineaux (character on *Breaking Bad*), 137
hydrofluoric acid, 14, 52–53
hyperreal, 89

identity politics, 8
ideological analysis, 8, 74, 133
immanence: and creativity, 79, 149; ethics and, 120, 134, 150–51; and ideology critique, 74; indeterminacy, 12, 48–49; and life, 79, 142–43; and mise-en-scène, 37, 98; politics of, 2–3, 74, 97, 115

improvisation, 32, 98–99, 113, 121, 127–31, 135, 137–38, 148
inadequate ideas, 73–77, 79, 119, 135, 149
inertia, 57–58, 77
intensive relations, 34–36, 39, 42, 46, 50–51, 54, 63–64, 69, 92, 153. *See also* extensive relations; mise-en-scène; thresholds
intertextual, 9, 13, 38
"I See You" (episode 308), 84

James, Tommy, and the Shondells, 154
Jameson, Fredric, 24, 93, 161n34, 169n7
Jesse Pinkman (character on *Breaking Bad*): affect and, 77–79, 97, 148; as the "black sheep," 45, 62, 89; and creativity, 149; drug use of, 49, 101, 107, 123; and Gale's murder, 64; homelessness and, 45, 58, 61; as moral center of series, 61, 79, 148; relationship with Jane, 49–51, 65; as surrogate son to Walt, 1, 65, 75–76, 102, 124, 138

"Kafkaesque" (episode 309), 48
Kant, Immanuel: Third Critique, 160n13
Keeling, Kara, 6, 30, 39
King, Robb Wilson, 67
King, Rodney, 28
kleptomania, 61, 131
Kodak film stock, 27
Kogonada, 86
Kracauer, Siegfried, 114–15
Krazy-8 (character on *Breaking Bad*), 81–82, 86, 104, 107–8, 119, 121, 132
Kubrick, Stanley, 108

Lacan, Jacques, 6, 75, 136
Lang, Fritz, 63, 111
language games, 119, 121, 123, 127, 134
Latinx, 40, 62, 119
Law, 34, 52, 61, 66, 77, 117, 125, 130, 141
Lawrence, D. H., 151–52
Leaves of Grass (Whitman), 14, 19, 23, 59, 75, 150
left/right cycles (in genres), 9, 80, 98–99, 147
Leone, Sergio, 38, 102, 129–30
Leonel Salamanca (character on *Breaking Bad*), 58–59, 84
LeRoy, Mervyn, 108
Life with Luigi (TV series), 21
lighting, 32, 57–60, 101–2, 107
lily of the valley, 124
line of flight, 24, 148, 149
"Live Free or Die" (episode 501), 47, 99, 130
Logan, Elliott, 10–11
long take, 10, 70
Losey, Joseph, 108
Los Pollos Hermanos, 48, 65, 114
Lotto ticket, 141
Lotz, Amanda, 5
low budget, 32–33, 119
Lucy Ricardo (character on *I Love Lucy*), 6, 140
Lumière brothers, 27
Lydia Rodarte-Quayle (character on *Breaking Bad*), 13, 130, 144
Lynch, David, 88
Lyons, Stewart, 58–59
Lyotard, Jean-François, 119–20

Mad Men (TV series), 7
"Madrigal" (episode 502), 84, 126, 130

Madrigal Corporation, 21, 84, 126
magic hour, 102
Mamma Roma (film), 55
Marie Schrader (character on *Breaking Bad*), 45, 58, 60–61, 63, 66, 75, 89, 116–17, 131–32, 138, 142
Marion Crane (character in *Psycho*), 14, 21, 38
mark/demark, 83–86
Martin, Adrian, 33
Marx, Karl, 127
masculinity, 21, 116, 128
Massumi, Brian, 134
master narrative, 118–21. *See also* language games
Max Arciniega (character on *Breaking Bad*), 123, 126
medium specificity, 5, 31, 162n11
Méliès, Georges, 27
melodrama, 60–62, 65–80, 118
meth. *See* drugs
Mexico, 1, 22–24, 112, 122, 152
Miami Vice (TV series), 27
Michael Corleone (character in *The Godfather*), 23, 125
Mike Ehrmantraut (character on *Breaking Bad*), 13–14, 47, 63–64, 84, 122, 125, 130
military-entertainment complex, 97
Miller, D. A., 10
Minnelli, Vincente, 74
mise-en-scène: and affect, 43–44, 66–70, 99; color in, 77–79; as intensive relay, 33–37, 41–42, 64, 66–68, 99; and lighting, 102–5; and melodrama, 68–80; musical values in, 68–71, 131; vs. narrative, 47–51, 153; as orchestration in the image, 32–33, 54–55, 99; and resonance, 12, 52, 99; and set design, 58–59; spectral resonance in, 14–21, 38–39, 102; as unfolding of virtual forces, 33–37, 41–42, 55, 69–70, 98–99, 120, 153. *See also* affect; haunted images; intensive relations; narrative; virtual
Mittell, Jason, 9–10
modernists, 88
modernity, 55–56, 68, 97, 110, 113, 115, 133
modernization, 40, 54, 94, 108, 126
molar, 19, 65
molecular, 152–53
Monkees, 156
montage, 27, 48, 55, 88, 125, 154, 156
Monument Valley, 102
morality, 50, 61, 64, 134, 148, 151; drugs and, 43; Nietzsche's critique of, 79–80, 151; radical evil, 112, 123–24; reactive, 13, 76, 79
MTM, 27
MTV, 27
Museum of Modern Art, 3
music video, 28, 48, 154, 170n14
Musketeers of Pig Alley, The (film), 55

narcocorrida, 48
narrative: in art cinema, 43–44; cause-effect chains in, 12, 34, 51–52, 71, 161n31; common sense and, 7; complexity, 9–10; and duration, 70–71; forking, 106–7; game play and, 116–20, 123–24; gaps (indeterminacy) in, 46–52, 120–21; improvisation in, 99; master, 118–20; vs. mise-en-scène, 11–12, 34–36, 44, 65; seriality and, 26, 68–70; and story line, 11
naturalism, 98
"Negro y Azul" (episode 207), 48, 84, 113

neoliberalism: and drugs, 8; and economic precarity, 7–8, 80, 134–35; and futurity, 113–14, 118; immaterial labor and, 136; just-in-time production and, 1, 53, 88, 121, 127, 129; and modes of experience, 8, 12, 51, 80, 129, 134–35, 141, 157; and post-Fordism, 8, 88; and postnetwork television, 7; privatization and, 147; and the white male, 80
neo-Nazis, 8, 75, 123, 125, 137–38, 147–48
neorealism, 7, 46, 49
New Hollywood, 9, 37
Newman, Michael, 68–69
new waves: in film history, 7, 41, 54–55, 162n11; on television, 7, 26
Nietzsche, Friedrich, 77, 79–80, 133–34, 151
No-Doze (character on *Breaking Bad*), 41–42
"No Más" (episode 301), 101
nonfascist life, 135, 148, 150, 154
Norman Bates (character in *Psycho*), 14, 19, 21, 39
norms, 31
"No-Rough-Stuff-Type Deal, A" (episode 107), 39, 41, 45, 61–62, 89, 130
Notorious (film), 82–83

objects: "bad," 26, 72; defamiliarization of, 83–89, 99–100; foregrounding of, 19, 47; Hitchcock and, 83; mise-en-scène and, 35–36, 54–55, 68, 153–54; object *a*, 136; outmoded, 92–96; out of place, 19; overlooked, 19; surrealism and, 83, 90–93
object world, 2, 6, 80–81, 83, 86, 142
O'Keeffe, Georgia, 65
"On a Clear Day" (song), 88
Once upon a Time in the West (film), 38–39, 130
ontology of the event, 120–21
Open, 153
Organization Man, 21
Our Mutual Friend, 143
outmoded, 5, 40, 92–95, 126
Outside, 19, 22–24, 143–44, 147–48
"Over" (episode 210), 86
"Ozymandias" (episode 514), 137–40, 152
"Ozymandias" (poem), 150, 152
Ozzie and Harriet (TV series), 21

Panagia, Davide, 11
Paramount, 33
paranoia, 21, 61, 63, 89, 107
Pasolini, Pier Paolo, 55
pastiche, 19. *See also* blank parody
Pat Garrett and Billy the Kid (film), 13
patriarchal, 35, 39, 51, 110, 126
Paul, Aaron, 48
Peckinpah, Sam, 13
pedagogy, 35, 75, 115
"Peekaboo" (episode 206), 86
Peirce, Charles S., 83. *See also* mark/demark
periodic table, 152
"Phoenix" (episode 212), 48–51
photogénie, 11, 162n11
"Pick Yourself Up" (song), 125
"Pilot" (episode 101), 45, 81, 86, 116, 121, 128
poetry, 75, 150
Point of View (TV series), 3
possible worlds, 12–13, 19
postmodernity, 56, 118–19, 156, 161n34. *See also* blank parody; pastiche
postnetwork, 4, 7, 25–26, 32, 56

precarity. *See* neoliberalism
preemptiveness, 135. *See also* decision making; futurity
"Problem Dog" (episode 407), 44, 77, 97
procedural, 6, 23, 27, 49
production design, 57, 67
production schedules, 32
profane illumination, 90, 94. *See also* Benjamin, Walter; surrealism
Psycho (film), 14–21, 39
psychoanalysis, 19, 31, 95, 136
psychotic, 21, 34–35, 51, 65

queer, 23, 72, 151
queer theory, 23

"Rabid Dog" (episode 512), 138–39
radical evil, 112, 123–24
Rancière, Jacques, 43–45, 65, 71, 73
Ray, Nicholas, 23, 32, 34, 37, 44, 71
Ray, Robert B., 9
reactive morality, 13, 76, 79
Rebel without a Cause (film), 71
reproductive futurism, 96, 119
residue, 12, 35, 51. *See also* surplus
resonance, 12, 19, 52, 120. *See also* mise-en-scène
ressentiment, 80, 149
rhythms, 56–57, 74, 131
Risky Business (film), 156–57
Rolling Stones, 41
Rope (film), 10
Rose, Charlie, 144
Rossellini, Roberto, 49

"Salud" (episode 410), 75, 112, 122, 124
Santa Muerte, 101
Sarris, Andrew, 162n5
"Say My Name" (episode 507), 13, 156
scale (in the image), 83, 152
Scorsese, Martin, 9, 41, 143
scriptwriting, 49. *See also* writers; writers' room
Searchers, The (film), 33, 102
Sedgwick, Eve Kosofsky, 150
segmentation, 68, 70
semiotic square, 21–25, 126
seriality, 10, 57, 68–70, 121, 139–40
serial television, 2, 5, 7, 10, 12, 30, 131, 140
set design, 39, 59
"Seven Thirty-Seven" (episode 201), 39
Shelley, Percy, 150, 152
Shining, The (film), 110
showrunner, 3, 7, 32
Sicily, 23
Simondon, Gilbert, 39
Sirk, Douglas, 71
sitcoms, 19
Six Feet Under (TV series), 7
Skyler White (character on *Breaking Bad*), 44–45, 51, 57–58, 60, 63, 66, 86, 116–17, 121, 138, 141–42
Slovis, John, 164n34
Smith, Adam, 133
Snowden, Edward, 100
society of the spectacle, 56, 126, 134, 154
Sopranos, The (TV series), 3–4, 7
spaghetti western, 33, 99, 129–31, 138
Spigel, Lynn, 3–4, 164n24
Spinoza, Baruch, 73, 79
Stevia, 144
Stiegler, Bernard, 56, 72, 121
studio set, 54, 58–59
"Sunset" (episode 306), 84
superlab, 93–94, 99
supplement (Derridean), 52, 129
surplus, 12, 19, 28, 51–52, 136

surrealism, 11, 53, 83–93, 96–100, 120
survival of the fittest, 133
Sympathy for the Devil (film), 41

Tarr, Bela, 43, 45
taste cultures, 5, 29. *See also* distinction
Taxi Driver (film), 9, 143–47
teaser, 12–14, 45, 47–48, 52, 54, 57, 65, 77, 102, 104, 126, 139, 144
technophilia, 130
teddy bear, 51, 101
television studies, 4–5, 8–9, 25–26, 29–30, 72, 120
televisuality, 27–28
Thaler, Richard H., 168n10
thalidomide, 94, 108
These Are the Damned (film), 108
They Live by Night (film), 23
Thomson, David, 162n5
thresholds, 33, 36, 62–65, 69
time-lapse photography, 131, 156
Times Square, 147
Tinker, Grant, 6
Todd Alquist (character on *Breaking Bad*), 14, 52–53, 75, 148
"To'hajiilee" (episode 513), 137, 140
Tomás Cantillo (character on *Breaking Bad*), 48, 107
Tony Soprano (character on *The Sopranos*), 140
Traffic in Souls (film), 55
Travis Bickle (character in *Taxi Driver*), 143–44
Truffaut, François, 162n7
Tsai Ming-liang, 55
Tucker, George Loane, 55
Tuco Salamanca (character on *Breaking Bad*), 39–42, 48, 62–63, 73, 129
Two or Three Things I Know about Her (film), 55, 144

Väliaho, Pasi, 39
Vamanos Pest Control, 13, 88
video game, 79, 97
Villarejo, Amy, 72, 75, 168n1
virtual: and affect, 43, 76–77; and crystal-image, 106, 110; as haunting, 2; and the image archive, 2, 38; and intensity, 34, 42; and the Open, 34, 148; and possible worlds, 12. *See also* actualization (of virtual)
Vive L'Amour (film), 55

Walter White (character on *Breaking Bad*): and arranged prison massacre, 125–26; arrest of, 137–38; bodily movements of, 128–29; character arc of, 1–2; death of, 140–41, 144, 147–49, 168n2; and DIY culture, 40–42, 99; excessive rationality of, 52–53, 74, 124, 132; as father/surrogate father, 51, 75–76, 101–2, 135, 138; and the fly, 12–21; and Heisenberg, 42, 47, 74, 153; improvisation and, 112–13, 121–22; Jane's death and, 48–51; and the Law, 61; and the lily of the valley, 124; masculine crisis, 13, 21, 116, 128; as monster, 53; murder of Gus Fring, 124; murder of Krazy-8, 81–82, 119; as psychotic, 21, 34–35, 65–66; role in Gale's murder, 63–64; as teacher, 108
Walter White Jr. (character on *Breaking Bad*), 44–45, 59, 75, 90, 128, 135, 139, 141
Weekend (film), 41
Welles, Orson, 44, 46, 106

western, 34, 67, 99, 102, 129–31, 138
White house. *See* domestic space
white male, 7–8, 29, 40, 80, 160n15
white privilege, 62
Whitman, Walt, 22, 113, 133, 150–51; *Leaves of Grass*, 14, 19, 23, 59, 75, 150
Williams, Linda, 68–69, 80
Williams, Raymond, 30
Willis, Gordon, 101
will-to-power, 133. *See also* Nietzsche, Friedrich
Winant, Scott, 165n8
"Windy" (song), 48
Winnebago, 81, 121, 138–39
Wire, The (TV series), 9–10, 68–69, 71, 90, 98
Wood, Robin, 162n6
"world memory," 139–40
writers, 10, 32, 38, 43, 69, 118, 147
writers' room, 10, 43, 118
Written on the Wind (film), 71
Wyler, William, 46

X-Files, The (TV series), 21

Zarzosa, Agustin, 73, 76–77
Zborowski, James, 5
zero-degree style, 72